m
media
MANUAL

Video Camera Techniques
Second Edition

media
MANUAL

Video Camera Techniques

Second Edition

Gerald Millerson

Focal Press
An imprint of Butterworth-Heinemann Ltd
Linacre House, Jordan Hill, Oxford OX2 8DP

Ɋ A member of the Reed Elsevier plc group

OXFORD LONDON BOSTON
MUNICH NEW DELHI SINGAPORE SYDNEY
TOKYO TORONTO WELLINGTON

First published 1983
Reprinted 1985, 1987 (with revision)
Second edition 1994

British Library Cataloguing in Publication Data

A catalogue record for this book is available from the British Library

ISBN 0 240 51376 2

Library of Congress Cataloguing in Publication Data

A catalogue record for this book is available from the Library of Congress

Printed and bound in Great Britain by
Biddles Ltd, Guildford and King's Lynn

Contents

Introduction

Thanks to ingenious design, many of today's video cameras allow you to simply 'point and press' – and still get worthwhile results even when shooting under the most difficult conditions. Controls that previously needed careful adjustment, are now often entirely AUTOMATIC!

So why do you need to study 'camera techniques'?
Well, there are several good reasons:

• OPERATIONAL SKILL — For smooth unobtrusive camerawork, you'll need to be able to handle your camera accurately and consistently. A hallmark of good picture-making is that it creates an immediate audience impact, while the underlying techniques remain unnoticed!

• ARTISTIC — What your audience looks at, and how they respond to what they are watching, will largely depend on the way you use your camera: the lens angle you select, how you arrange the subject within the picture frame, how you adjust focusing, move your camera . . . and so on.

• PICTURE QUALITY — Auto-controls can be a great help, particularly where the action is very unpredictable. But as we shall see, they cannot make artistic judgments for you. Even a slight alteration in exposure or camera position can alter the entire mood of a picture.

• COORDINATION — Whether you are working alone, or part of a multi-camera team, your techniques can directly influence all other aspects of the production: the success of the script, performance, editing, even lighting and sound treatment.

This book has been specially devised to provide you with a straightforward step-by-step guide to effective video camerawork of professional standards. You'll find here, camera handling and picture making from basics to advanced techniques. It will help you to master camera operation and quickly develop your own style and imaginative skills. It's a fascinating study!

Acknowledgements
As well as acknowledging the permission of the Director of Engineering of the British Broadcasting Corporation for permission to publish the original book (TV CAMERA OPERATION), I want to express my appreciation of the encouragement of various colleagues. Particularly, I want to thank Bob Longman (formerly Controller, Engineering and Operations, BBC Television), and Bob Warman (then Technical Manager), who with many years' experience of TV camerawork, appraised its manuscript.

Gerald Millerson

Video Cameras

Today's video cameras come in many shapes and forms; from peanut-sized surveillance units, to large heavy duty studio cameras.

Consumer camera systems

Used mainly for home videos and low-budget program-making, consumer camera systems with their in-built recording facilities, offer a wide range of program-making opportunities.

Palmcorders are increasingly popular for everyday use. Thanks to their small size and easy-to-use controls, they are extremely straightforward to operate, and results are very satisfactory for less exacting program making.

Compact video cameras include numerous automatic controls that help to make shooting easier. Picture quality can be remarkably good, so that they are sometimes used for news gathering, where expensive equipment might be hazarded.

Full-size consumer cameras are more robust, and include various refinements approaching professional quality performance.

Professional camera systems

ENG/SNG/EFP cameras are used in the field for *news gathering* (electronic or satellite), and for *electronic field production* when shooting location drama or documentaries. These lightweight units are extremely adaptable, for they can be supported on the shoulder as you move around, or mounted on a rolling-tripod in the studio.

Studio cameras on the other hand, which provide state-of-the-art performance, are comparatively heavy and bulky, owing to the high performance zoom lens and large viewfinder they carry. Consequently, they are usually fitted to a heavy duty mounting, such as a pedestal .

While *lightweight* camera systems may be self-contained, and include their own videotape recorders, the *studio camera* is normally cable-linked to a central control point (*camera control unit* or *base station*), where picture quality is continually monitored and adjusted by a specialist operator (*shader, vision operator*), rather than rely on somewhat unpredictable automatic facilities.

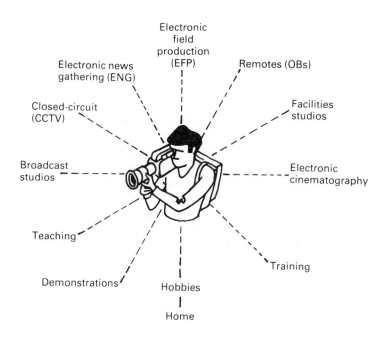

Electronic
field
production
(EFP)

Electronic news
gathering (ENG)

Remotes (OBs)

Closed-circuit
(CCTV)

Facilities
studios

Broadcast
studios

Electronic
cinematography

Teaching

Demonstrations

Hobbies

Training

Home

A range of shooting conditions
The versatility of video cameras makes them adaptable to all forms
of program-making.

Meet your Camera

Most of us feel awkward when handling a piece of technical equipment for the first time. Even when we are familiar enough with similar devices, there will usually be some changes in design or layout that can leave us uncertain. Although the video camera is technically complex, it is surprisingly straightforward to operate. At first you may feel a little apprehensive, but nowadays even modestly priced equipment is pretty foolproof, and remarkably rugged. The answer to most difficulties is *practice*. And don't forget the old adage: '*When all else fails, read the instructions*'!

You can always check the results

You don't need to be 'technically-minded' to use a video camera successfully. There will of course, be those odd occasions when things go wrong, or you don't get the results you expected, but the video camera has one outstanding advantage. You can replay the videotape immediately to check your work on the spot; either using the camera viewfinder, or a picture monitor. This enables you to review what you have just shot and to correct any errors – unlike *film*, which has to be processed and projected before you can confirm that all is well.

Remember, the video camera is simply an electronic device that continuously produces pictures as long as it is powered. Videotape is cheap, and can be re-used over and over, so you can shoot generously where necessary, without wasting stock.

Successful picture making

To get the best out of your camera, you need to use it selectively. Simply setting controls to 'automatic' and pointing your camera at the scene may produce great results, but the magic of good cameracraft comes from a blend of skills:

• Easy familiarity with the camera's controls, so that you can operate them confidently and accurately.

• An eye for pictorial opportunities; selecting a good viewpoint, composing effective shots.

• And then there are those less tangible qualities that the best camera operators have, including dexterity, stamina, patience, and a good memory!

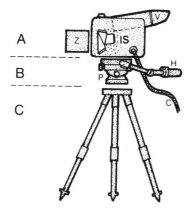

The video/TV camera
The camera unit consists of:

A. The camera head   Z, zoom lens. IS, image sensors (CCDs). V, viewfinder.
C, camera cable (taking technical supplies to the camera, and the resultant video
to the camera control unit/CCU). A quick-release *wedge-mount* under the head
slides into a corresponding recessed plate on the panning head.

B. The panning head (pan head)   This enables the camera head to tilt and turn
(*pan*) smoothly. These movements can be restrained by deliberately introduced
friction (*drag*), and can be *locked off* to hold the head rigid. *Tilt balance* positions
the head horizontally, preventing it being nose- or tail-heavy. One or two
attached *pan (panning) handles* (H) enable the cameraman to direct and control
the camera head.

C. The camera mounting   This can take many forms, e.g. camera-clamp,
monopod, tripod, pedestal, crane.

13

Camera Systems

There are two basic approaches to video camera system design –
- *One-piece* or *integrated units.*
- *Modular or convertible systems.*

One-piece units

Here the camera is usually self-contained, and may either be a *camcorder* fitted with its own integral videocassette recording unit (*VCR*), or connected by a cable to a small portable videotape recorder nearby. (The recorder may be carried in a shoulder or back-pack, or on a small wheeled trolley-pack.)

You can make a limited number of changes to an integrated camera system. For example, you can –
- Replace the zoom lens with another having a different range.
- Clip on a small *LCD* color monitor screen, to supplement the eyepiece viewfinder fitted to the camera, or use a stand-alone picture monitor.
- Plug in a high-quality microphone.
- The camera's power can be supplied by an internal or attached *on-board* battery, or by a separate videotape recorder unit's supply.

Modular systems

Modular systems are extremely versatile. They allow you to convert your camera arrangements in various ways, depending on the type of production and shooting conditions. The *camera head* is the heart of the system, and it can be used with a range of different accessories:

- *The lens system* – From compact lightweight types to large state-of-art units. Usually a zoom lens, but sometimes *prime lenses* (fixed focal length) or special purpose types may be used instead. Effects filters may be added to modify the lens image in various ways.
- *The types of camera controls* – You may make lens adjustments *(focus, lens aperture, focal length)* on the lens-system itself, or use separate controls attached to the *pan bars (panning handles).* Alternatively, some or all of these adjustments may be controlled remotely *(I.R. control; CCU).*
- *The viewfinder* – An adjustable *eyepiece* design, which can be repositioned on either side of the camera. A black and white or color monitor attached to the top of the camera. A clip-on *LCD screen.* Sometimes an additional high-grade picture monitor is more convenient.

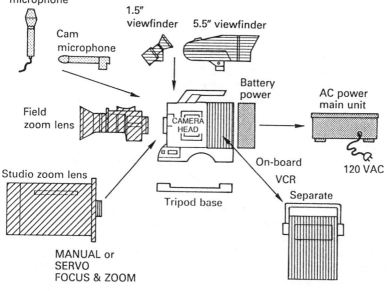

Hand microphone

Cam microphone

1.5" viewfinder

5.5" viewfinder

Field zoom lens

CAMERA HEAD

Battery power

AC power main unit

120 VAC

Studio zoom lens

On-board VCR

Separate

Tripod base

MANUAL or SERVO FOCUS & ZOOM

Modular cameras
Various features can be attached to the camera head to suit the type of production.

Creating the Picture

To create a television or video picture, the image from the camera lens is focused onto the light sensitive surface of a sensor of some kind – either the target of a *camera tube*, or more usually nowadays, a solid-state device called a *CCD* (*charge-coupled device*). Here a pattern of electrical voltages develops, which corresponds to the light and shade in each part of the image. As these charges are scanned in a series of regular horizontal lines, their values are read off to form a fluctuating voltage – the *video signal*.

This is conveyed to the TV receiver or video monitor where an electron beam scans across the screen phosphors of the picture tube in exact step with the camera, thanks to a series of regular *sync (synchronizing) pulses*. Because this scanning beam's strength varies in intensity with the original video signal, it traces out a pattern of light and shade, which we interpret as a picture of the original scene.

In order to produce *color* pictures, the camera lens' image is split into three identical paths, where color filters analyze the scene into its color proportions, producing corresponding '*R. G. B.*' (red, green, and blue) video signals. At the TV receiver (monitor), the three versions activate respective phosphors which glow in these *color primaries*, appearing intermixed to the eye, and creating a full-color image. Professional cameras use three separate CCDs for this color analysis process, but simpler video cameras get by with a multistripe color filter over a single CCD.

The CCD image sensor
The CCD image sensor has many advantages over a camera tube. It costs less, is robust, small (typically $2/3$ or $1/2$ in. diagonal), uses low power, and has a long life. CCD sensors are very stable, and less easily damaged by over-exposure to light sources or specular reflections. Certain inherent limitations (e.g. producing a vertical smear on bright lights/speculars), have been largely overcome in more advanced designs.

Although unimpressive enough to the eye, the CCD is an extremely sophisticated electronic device. Broadly speaking, it consists of a flat plate, surfaced with hundreds of thousands of tiny photo-diodes. These are arranged in close horizontal rows, corresponding to the TV system's scanning lines.

Each photodiode has its associated transistor switch. When a specially generated pulse is applied to this local switch, that element's charge is transferred to a nearby electronic *shift register*. The charges that are collected there, are successively read off (*stepped*) to provide the *video*.

A

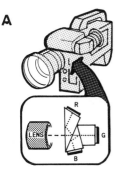

How video works
A. Just behind the camera lens a *prism block* with color filters (dichroics), is used to produce three images, corresponding to the red, green and blue in the scene. Attached to these prisms are three *CCD light sensors*. A pattern of charges builds up on their tiny elements, corresponding to the light and shade in their color images.

B

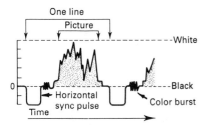

B. The pattern of charges on each CCD is read out in a regular series of lines, to produce a *video signal*. Thanks to *synchronizing pulses* the three CCDs are scanned exactly in step (synchronous).

One line
Picture
-----White
0
-----Black
Horizontal sync pulse
Color burst
Time

The video signal

C

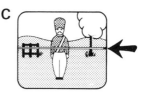

C. If we look at a single line as the system reads across the picture. . .

D

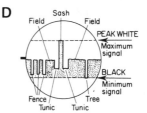

Sash
Field   Field
PEAK WHITE
Maximum signal
BLACK
Minimum signal
Fence   Tree
Tunic   Tunic

D. . . . we see how the strength of the video signal fluctuates with the tones at each moment of the scan.

E

R B
G

E. The TV receiver is fed simultaneously with the three different video signals – red, green, blue.

The screen of the *picture tube* in the TV receiver or monitor, has a pattern of three different phosphors on its inner surface. Streams of electrons are controlled by the RGB video signals. As they scan across their respective sets of phosphors. these glow red, green, or blue, and build up a color picture.

The Camera Lens

There are three features of your camera lens that you need to know about to use it effectively:

- How its *focal length* affects the picture and the camera's handling.
- The way *focusing* can influence the audience's concentration.
- What happens when you adjust the lens *aperture (iris; f-stop)*.

We shall be discussing the practical aspects of these features in detail later. For the moment, let's take a look at the way you make these adjustments.

The zoom lens

Most video cameras are fitted with a *zoom* lens. As you have probably discovered, this provides a variable coverage; from a wide-angle setting, that takes in a large area of the scene, to a narrow-angle or *telephoto* setting showing a much closer, more restricted view.

The 'zoom' effect is achieved by adjusting certain elements within the lens barrel. Repositioning these alters the lens' effective *focal length*. When zoomed right in to the *telephoto* setting, the focal length is at its longest. Zoomed right out to the wide angle position, the focal length is shortest.

You control zooming *manually* by turning a knob on the lens barrel, or a hand control on a *pan-bar (panning handle)*. (The latter may be a direct cable or servo-motor controlled). On many cameras, a two-way *rocker switch* on the right side of the lens assembly, controls a motor which drives the zoom in and out. The *power zoom* speed varies with the switch pressure.

The focus control

To focus the subject, either the entire lens system is moved in/out, or internal lens elements are repositioned while the lens-to-light sensor (CCD) distance remains constant. The simplest method of focusing, is to rotate a *ring* on the lens barrel, where a scale shows the focused distance. Alternatively, a *remote focus* control on a pan-bar may be used to adjust focus, or a *focus knob* fixed at the side of the camera.

Adjusting the lens aperture

Looking inside the lens barrel, you will see a multi-bladed *diaphragm* or *iris*. This adjusts the *lens aperture*, and controls the overall amount of light passing through the lens system, to fall onto the CCD pick-up device. It is altered by turning a ring on the lens barrel, against a scale which is calibrated in *f-stops* or *transmission numbers*. Alternatively, remote controls may be fitted on a pan-bar.

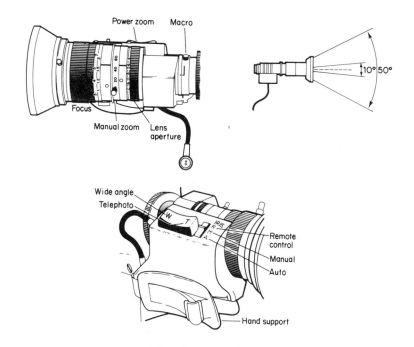

The zoom lens

This has adjustable focus, iris and focal length (lens angle). Altering the focal length varies the lens coverage. Changing it while on shot produces 'zooming': zooming in as the focal length increases, and zooming out as it decreases.

The focal length may be adjusted manually (knob on lens barrel), or with a motor system (power zoom) operated with a rocker-switch, from wide angle to telephoto (narrow angle).

Nearby switches also control the iris (lens aperture): auto, manual, and remote control.

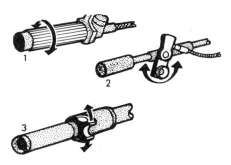

Forms of zoom control

On studio cameras:
1. Twist-grip.
2. Hand-crank.
3. Thumb-lever.

Panning handle controls

When a camera is fitted to a mounting, the lens is usually adjusted with extension controls: *zoom control* (1–twist-grip) fixed to the left panning handle; *focus control* (2–hand-crank) to the right.

19

The Viewfinder

Your camera's viewfinder is a vital link in good picture-making:

- It shows exactly how much of the scene is visible in the shot – to ensure that no unwanted subjects (e.g. the microphone, or bystanders) are accidentally included within the picture.
- It enables you to arrange the shot accurately within the frame, composing the picture for maximum impact.
- It shows you exactly how much of the shot is *sharply focused*.
- It helps you to judge *exposure* and *picture quality* as you shoot.
- It can help when matching shots to other cameras; e.g. by showing their outputs combined with your own picture.
- Particularly when working in the field, it can be useful to monitor video-tape playback of the scene you have just recorded.

Types of Viewfinder

Most video cameras are fitted with an electronic viewfinder of some kind. *The eyepiece type* — This is fitted with a small magnified black and white picture tube (typically 1.5 in./38 mm diam.). You hold its flexible eyepiece against one eye, adjusting a compensatory lens to suit your eyesight. The viewfinder may be repositioned on top or on either side of the camera.

The open-screen type — Fitted on top of the camera head you use both eyes to view this 5 or 7 in. monitor (12.5 or 18 cms.) so it is less tiring to watch for long periods. Tilting the viewfinder makes it easier to see at different camera heights. A hooded visor keeps stray light from falling onto its picture. *Monochrome* viewfinders are generally used, as they allow more critical focusing. But color versions do have advantages – allowing you to check the picture's color quality, assess color relationships, pick out color clues (e.g. a particular team's shirts in a ball game), avoid colored *lens flares*.

The LCD screen — Small liquid crystal displays are thin, lightweight, and use little power. Although clarity and color quality are not high, the LCD screen is often much more convenient than a color monitor in the field.

Viewfinder Adjustments

The main viewfinder controls usually include *screen brightness*, *screen focus, contrast* (which increases/decreases tonal differences), *crispener* (which emphasizes viewfinder detail, to make focus adjustments easier to see). A color viewfinder also includes color strength adjustments (*saturation*). Remember, these controls only affect the viewfinder's picture, leaving your camera's output unaffected.

Typical camera indicators

Various types of indicators are fitted to video cameras, including the following;

• Autofocusing zone select	Shows whether the *autofocus* is controlled by a small central area of the shot, or the nearest subject in the scene.
• Back light exposure	A system that opens the lens aperture an arbitrary stop or so above the *auto-iris* setting, to improve exposure against bright backgrounds.
• Battery alarm.	A warning light showing that the *battery* is OK, or that it is getting exhausted.
• Boost setting.	Shows amount of *video amplification* (gain) being used.
• Call light.	Indicator showing that someone on a *private-wire* system wishes to talk to the camera operator .
• Date and time indicator.	Displays details on screen, for insertion into picture.
• End of tape warning.	Shows that only e.g. 1 minute of tape remains.
• Exposure indicator	A light or pattern superimposed on the viewfinder (e.g. '*zebra stripes*') showing when the picture is technically over or under exposed.
• Full-auto indicator.	Shows that camera is in *fully automatic mode* (i.e. *auto-iris, auto-focus,* etc.).
• Low light level warning.	Insufficient light falling onto the CCD, causing underexposure. (Open iris and/or increase boost.)
• Manual aperture setting.	Shows that the lens is manually controlled.
• Manual focus correct.	The lens is manually focused, and correctly adjusted.
• Moisture and dew.	Indicates if the VCR system has been subjected to moisture (e.g. condensation) which would ruin the recording (affecting *stiction* of tape on the scanning capstan).
• Filter selection	Shows which filter in filter wheel has been selected.
• Playback.	Indicates that the VCR is replaying the tape.
• Shutter speed.	Shows which shutter speed has been selected.
• Tape speed selected.	Shows whether normal tape speed or half-speed has been selected on the VCR.
• Tally light.	A cue light showing that the camera is recording; or when used with a switcher unit, that this camera has been selected 'on-air'.
• Time indicator.	Shows the running time (elapsed time/tape time used) and/or the time remaining on the cassette.
• Titles.	A small character generator that provides titles, which can be superimposed on the picture.
• Video/audio recording.	Indicates that the VCR is recording picture and sound.
• Video level.	A display superimposed on the viewfinder,showing the video signal's strength and exposure.
• Viewfinder markers.	Markings on the screen showing the exact center, and the *safe area* within which all important information should be contained.
• White balance.	Shows if the color balance (color temperature) adjustment is satisfactory.

21

Small-Format Cameras

Hand-held small-format or 'consumer' video camcorders have now become a regular part of everyday life. Their ingenious design and ever-increasing facilities offer us a wide range of picture-making opportunities – from home video recording to educational and training programs. Although the single CCD used in small-format cameras limits picture definition and color fidelity, picture quality has now improved so much, that the clips of eyewitness 'amateur video' often included in newscasts, can compare remarkably well with shots from regular three-CCD ENG broadcast cameras.

The video light
The small *video light* attached to the top of the camera is invaluable when you cannot arrange suitable lighting. While working in poor light, it can provide you with your main light source. Where there is sufficient illumination around but it is over-contrasty, the video light will illuminate shadows, and reduce harsh tonal contrasts. However, the video light is uncontrollable, and liable to produce strong specular reflections in shiny surfaces as it moves around with the camera. It can dazzle and distract.

The camera microphone
The *camera microphone* attached to small-format cameras, may be fixed or set on a small telescopic rod or 'boom'. Although useful when working by yourself, this sound pickup arrangement does have disadvantages, so it may be preferable to use a separate microphone of better quality, plugged into an input jack on the camera instead. Its main limitations are that it tends to overhear camera noise from the zoom and auto-focus mechanisms. And it is often too far from the sound source.

The need for indicators
When you are using this type of camera, you do not have the backup assistance of a *CCU* or *base station*. So small-format cameras are provided with a variety of indicators to show you equipment data and settings at a glance. Some of these indicators are visible within the viewfinder as you shoot, others are located along the sides and rear of the camera. They have several purposes:
- *Reminders* – e.g. Showing the focal length/lens-angle being used.
- *Warnings* – e.g. Of the amount of tape left, or battery life remaining.
- *Guides* – e.g. A zebra-stripe light pattern in the viewfinder, showing areas in the picture approaching *over-exposure* (maximum video level).

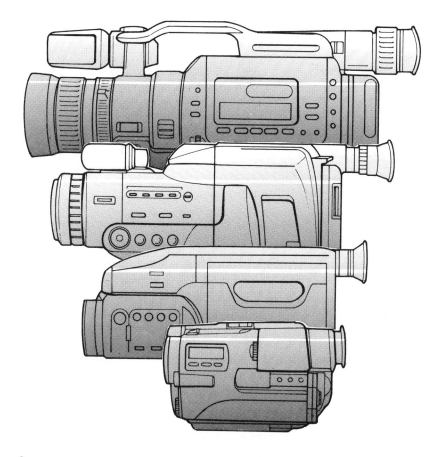

Consumer cameras
A wide range of excellent designs is
available in the consumer market,
from *palmcorders* to *lightweight*
systems.

Portable/Lightweight Cameras

These are the familiar all-purpose 'portable' or 'lightweight' camera units which are used for news-gathering (ENG), shooting on location (electronic field production; EFP), and for small studio work. Performance ranges from high-grade single-CCD types, to 3-CCD forms which produce pictures of top broadcast quality.

Formats
The main advantage of this type of unit, is its flexibility. You can carry it around on a shoulder, mount it on a tripod, a pedestal, or a jib arm, equally effectively.

Demountable or modular forms of portable camera can be fitted with different lenses, viewfinders, controls (focus, zoom) to suit the type of production you are shooting.

You can use the portable camera unit –
• Cabled directly to a switcher (vision mixer), with other cameras,
• Cabled to a separate videotape recorder,
• With a small attached (dockable) form of videotape recorder — typically Hi8, S-VHS, Betacam SP, or MII types.

When the camera is linked to a base station (where video and sound are recorded or passed on to e.g. a news center), it may be connected to a long cable (triax or fiber-optic types) – or for greater mobility, fitted with a transmitter (radio; infra-red).

Power flexibility
Portable cameras can be powered by several methods: from an attached on-board battery pack, a battery belt, a separate videotape recorder's power supply, a heavy-duty battery in a shoulder pack or on a cart or trolley (trolley-pack), a car battery. Or you can use regular utility (mains) supplies, via an AC power adapter. Typical supplies required by the camera are 12 (11-17)Vdc, or 115-120 (220/240)Vac.

Working set-up
You can use portable cameras either as self-contained stand-alone units, or linked together with other cameras (portable or studio types) to form a camera crew. The camera head itself contains all the picture generating, synchronizing, and control circuitry required to produce high quality pictures. When used in conjuction with other cameras however, the group is genlocked instead with a communal synchronizing signal – otherwise their pictures would jump or appear displaced or tear, when intercut or mixed.

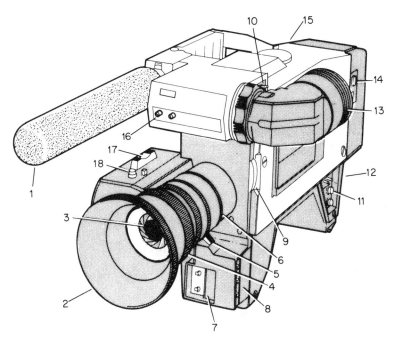

Parts of the camera

Camera designs vary, but the following are typical facilities found in the video camera:

1. Microphone – electret unidirectional
2. Lens hood
3. Lens aperture (iris) – f/1.6 max.
4. Focus control
5. Manual zoom control
6. Aperture control
7. White balance adjust; black adjust
8. Video gain (0 dB, 6 dB, 12 dB), color bars, camera standby/operate switch
9. Color compensation filter – 3200 K, 5600 K, 5600 K + 12.5% ND, closed
10. Viewfinder adjustable – 1.5 in (37 mm) with LED indicators
11. Power selection, intercom, audio monitoring jack
12. Camera back. VTR connector, video output camera cable, monitor video output, gen-lock connection for multi-camera setups
13. Eyepiece
14. Snap-on battery pack
15. Side of camera: mike input connector, external d.c. socket
16. Viewfinder controls
17. Power zoom switch
18. Auto-iris on/off

25

Studio Cameras

Generally found in larger production centers, the *studio* or *production camera* is a *state-of-the-art* piece of equipment, producing pictures of the highest broadcast quality. It is normally linked with others in a multi-camera setup – for newscasts, panel shows, interviews, drama, comedy shows, etc. When used outside the studio (e.g. at public events), it is usually set up at fixed viewpoints overlooking the action.

The camera chain
There are important differences between this type of camera and those we met earlier. *It is not self-contained.* It forms part of a centralized system.

Each camera is cabled to an associated *camera control unit (CCU)* outside the studio. (In digital systems, called a *base station.*) This cable carries all supplies, video, synchronizing pulses, intercom, etc., to and from the camera. The camera's video signals are processed at the CCU, and adjusted there or at an extension *vision control desk*, by a specialist operator (*shader, vision operator*) who continually assesses each camera's performance (artistically and technically). Where necessary, controls adjust *exposure, gamma, picture black level (sit), color balance*. This ensures that intercut cameras' shots are consistent, and matched in color and tonal fidelity.

The cameras' outputs are then routed to a *production switcher* for selection by the *director*, and subsequently passed on to a VTR channel. Sound pickup follows a quite separate route from studio microphone to the VTR soundtrack, via an *audio mixer or control console*.

Facilities
The studio camera is fitted with a large zoom lens system, which is adjusted electronically by servo controls on the *panning handles (pan bars)*. Typically, the *focus control* is attached to the left one, and the *zoom control* to the right handle. *Exposure* is controlled at the CCU or *vision control desk*.

The range of angles covered by the *studio zoom lens* is designed to suit subject distances within the studio. *Field zoom lenses* used on remotes (on location) generally have much narrower lens angles; otherwise very distant subjects would appear too small in the shot.

The *viewfinder* on studio cameras is an open-screen 5 in. or 7 in. type. Wearing earphones or a headset, the camera operator can hear the director's *intercom (talkback)* in one ear, while listening to the *program sound* in the other. Intercom circuits can be communal or switched private wires to individuals (e.g. to the *shader/vision operator; lighting director*).

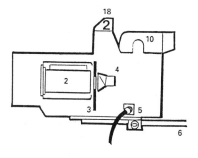

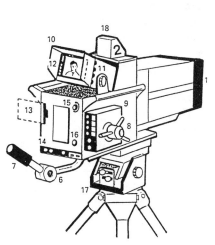

The camera head

1. Lens hood (sun shade, ray shade).
2. Zoom lens.
3. Filter wheel.
4. Prism block (beam splitter) with CCD image sensors
5. Camera cable.
6. Adjustable panning handle (pan handle, pan bar).
7. Twist-grip zoom control.
8. Focus control (many cameras use a control mounted on a panning handle – RHS).
9. Shot box (mounted on the camera head, or on a panning handle – RHS).
10. Monochrome viewfinder (perhaps with magnifying lens).
11. Viewfinder controls (including hi-peaker, crispening image detail).
12. Indicators: mimic tally light, lens-aperture indicator (*f*-stop), zoom lens setting (focal length/lens angle), etc.
13. Camera card clip.
14. Headset jack points (intercom and program) with volume controls. Mixed viewfinder feeds switch.
15. Zoom lens range-extender switch.
16. Call button (contacts shader/video control).
17. Camera mounting head (panning head/pan head), with drag adjustment for tilt and pan action, and tilt/pan locks. Also tilt fore-aft balance adjustment.
18. Tally light with camera number, illuminated when camera selected to line on switcher.

Hand-holding the Camera

There are several regular ways of supporting your camera:
- Hold it in your hands.
- Rest it on your shoulder.
- Use some kind of body support.
- Affix it to some kind of mounting.

For brief shots, or when shooting on the move, it is often sufficient to hand-hold the camera – provided you grip it properly.

- *Palmcorders* are best held with both hands: your right hand through the support strap on the zoom lens; your left hand under the camera's body. Although some cameras are fitted with an *electronic image stabilizer* don't rely on this device to compensate for wavering one-handed operation.

- *Compact* models with large lenses are best steadied with the fingers of your left hand under the lens mount, and your right in the support strap.

- *Portable* cameras have a molded saddle-type base or a pad which rests on your shoulder. You steady the camera by pressing it against your cheek. Your left hand will be on the lens barrel controlling focus, while the right is through the support strap, operating the zoom controls.

When hand-holding the camera, you soon learn the trick of not gripping it so tightly that every breath and body movement shakes the picture. Remember that particularly when fitted with a zoom lens, lamp, videocassette recorder and batteries, even a 'lightweight' camera feels increasingly heavier with time, and muscles tire.

Moving around

It is not easy to move around while shooting, without pictures shaking, bouncing, or leaning over to one side. The best method is to make sure that you tuck your elbows in to your body, and adopt a slightly-bent knee stance to cushion each step. Always keep both eyes open – watching the viewfinder picture, while looking around to check out for obstacles.

It can be particularly hazardous when shooting as you walk *backwards*, and it's advisable if you are working with another person (e.g. who is probably holding a camera light, a microphone, and recording equipment) to have them guide you; perhaps with a hand on your shoulder or belt.

Whenever you need to *pan* the camera round in an arc to follow action in a *panning shot*, stand mid-way with your feet astride and a straight back, and twist your body from the waist. If you are shooting a panoramic view of a scene, take care not to pan too quickly, or you will reduce everything to an indecipherable blur.

Very often, you will be able to find a firm support nearby, to rest your camera and steady your shots; as you can see in the examples opposite.

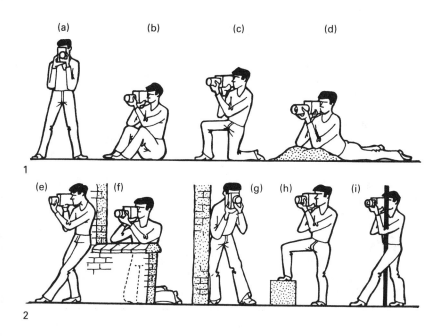

Hand-held supports

Any camera shake causes the picture to weave and hop about, so it is essential to hold it as rigidly as possible. Grip your camera firmly (but not too tightly) with your eye against the eyepiece and both arms tucked well in. Various techniques help to steady the camera:

1. Stable body positions: (a) legs braced apart; (b) seated, elbow on knees; (c) kneeling; (d) ground support.
2. Nearby supports: (e) back to wall; (f) resting on low wall, fence, railings, car etc.; (g) leaning side against wall; (h) foot on step or box; (i) resting against post.

Supporting the Camera

To help steady the camera while you are shooting, several ingenious devices have evolved.

Simple camera supports
Although very basic, the trick of hanging *a string or chain* from beneath the camera, and trapping its lower end under your foot, does give the camera a certain amount of stability as you pull up on it.

Better still, use a *monopod*. This is a telescopic tube that screws beneath the camera, and serves as a prop. It is simple, lightweight, and cheap; but take care to always keep it *upright*, to avoid sloping horizons!

Body supports
Several types of body brace or shoulder harness are available. Here the camera rests on your shoulder, and a brace below is supported on the chest or in a receptacle on your belt. This arrangement does relieve the weight of a shoulder-mounted camera. But some people find this kind of support restrictive, and feel that it is difficult to avoid 'breathing bounce'.

Stabilizers
Ingenious stabilizing harnesses such as the *Steadicam* or the *Panaglide* can produce steady shots even under the most extreme conditions. An elaborate spring-counterbalanced harness allows you to walk, run and climb, yet produce smooth-flowing picture sequences. A viewfinder fitted to the harness, allows the operator to control the shots. Unfortunately, this type of harness, which can support full-size portable video and film cameras, is rather heavy and cumbersome, so shooting for long periods can prove tiring.

The *Steadicam Junior* stabilizer on the other hand, is a lightweight and surprisingly compact device. Normally held in one hand as you move around, it takes the shake and shudder out of even wide camera movements. Designed for 8 mm, Hi8, and VHS-C camcorders weighing up to about 4 lb (1.8 kg), it consists of a small camera platform supported on a gimballed handle, with two folding arms. The stabilizer can also be rested on the shoulder as a comfortable brace, or folded beneath the camera when you are using a tripod.

Its lightweight 3½ in. LCD viewfinder screen, is treated to reduce light reflections. An on-board camera light (*Obie light*) is color balanced to 3200° K, and is useful to soften shadows, and to provide extra illumination in those awkward corners.

Simple camera supports

(1) String or chain support: attached beneath camera, trapped under one foot and pulled upwards.
(2) Monopod: single-leg telescopic tube, or pole.

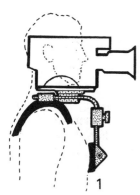

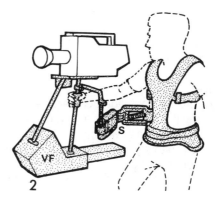

Camera stabilizers

To increase the stability of hand-held cameras:

1. Some form of shoulder-support/ shoulder-pod, brace or body harness may be worn.

2. In the *Steadicam* system, an elaborate spring-stabilized harness (S) is used to hold the camera steady, even during violent movement. A 4-inch electronic viewfinder (adjustable position) is fitted to the support arm (VF).

The Steadicam-Jr

A compact balanced support, that holds the camera rock steady, even when you are moving around. It incorporates a video light and an LCD color monitor.

31

The Mounting Head

The *mounting head* (*panning head*) that attaches the camera head to the main camera mounting, does two things:
* It supports the camera securely.
* It allows you to swivel the camera from side to side (*panning*), and to tilt it up and down (*tilting*) to follow the action

On lightweight cameras a *panning handle* (*pan bar*) fixed to the right side of the mounting head is used to control camera movements, while your left hand adjusts the *focus* ring on the *lens barrel*. On larger cameras, two panning handles are normally fitted, with extended *focus* and *zoom* controls attached.

The camera may screw directly onto the head, or have a quick-release *wedge plate* underneath it, which slides into a recessed plate on the mounting head.

Balance
Always ensure that your camera is correctly *balanced* on the head, particularly if you have just added/removed a prompter. Otherwise, if you forget to apply the *vertical lock*, the camera will drop forwards or backwards, badly jarring the system. A tripod might even overbalance! Many mounting heads include a *balance indicator* to aid forward/backward adjustment of the camera's position.

Drag
Ideally, the mounting head should offer a certain amount of resistance as you pan and tilt. Too much *drag*, and moves will be bumpy and erratic, especially on long-focus (narrow-angle lens settings). Too little, and accurate framing is more difficult. You may overshoot at the end of a pan or tilt.

If you want to hold the camera absolutely still (e.g. to avoid movement when shooting a graphic, or when leaving the camera unattended), use the head's horizontal and vertical *lock* controls. Over-tightening the *drag* controls can cause wear.

Types of head
There are several regular forms of mounting head:
* The *friction head* which relies on the pressure between parts to steady pan and tilt movements. The weakness of this design is that at the start and end of a slow pan, uneven pressure may cause sudden sticking, and jerk the shot.
* The *fluid effect head* has low-friction nylon dampers, which provide resistance.
* The *fluid head* is widely used with lightweight cameras. This has layers of high-viscosity silicon fluid which dampen head movement, and produce very smooth action that is unaffected by temperature changes. Internal springs offer drag resistance.
* The *cam heads* used for heavier cameras, have internal cams or cylinders to control movement.

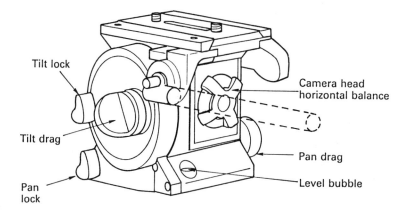

Tilt lock

Tilt drag

Pan
lock

Camera head
horizontal balance

Pan drag

Level bubble

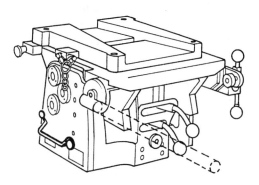

Camera mounting heads

Attached to the top of the camera mounting (e.g. a tripod) the *camera mounting head* or *panning head* allows the camera head to be tilted and panned, or locked off in any position. One or two *pan bars (panning handles)* are attached to steady and direct the camera.

Here are two widely used forms (by *Vinten*), using fluid drag control:
1. For lightweight cameras
2. For heavier camera units with larger zoom lenses and prompters.

The Camera Tripod

The tripod's three-legged stand is able to provide a very rigid support for your camera, even when shooting under difficult conditions. It is compact and portable, and its height is adjustable (e.g. 2 to 6 ft (55 cm to 2 m)).

Design details
The tripod's telescopic legs which are independently extendable, are usually constructed from metal-alloy or carbon fiber. There are many variations on tripod design, from simple low cost systems to very adaptable sophisticated arrangements. The best have bracing supports between a central column and each leg for added rigidity. To prevent the tripod's feet from slipping, they normally have either rubber-pads for smooth ground, or spikes (screw-out or retractable) for rough surfaces.

Attached to the top of the tripod, is a *panning head* to which the camera is attached. Its bubble-type *level indicator (spirit level)* helps to ensure that you have set up the tripod absolutely vertically – otherwise horizontals will appear to tilt as you pan around!

Altering camera height
You can alter the *camera's height* by moving the tripod's *central column* up and down. This may simply involve loosening a retaining screw to reposition the column; or there may be a *hand crank* that you turn to raise and lower it. A further system uses a *pneumatic* center column, which allows you to make smooth 'on air' adjustments to the camera height – unlike the other methods. Another way of altering the camera's height, is to adjust the *length* of the tripod's legs – either similarly, or to different extents when setting it up on a stairway or sloping surface.

Beware!
At maximum height, tripods may become top-heavy and over-balance. Always set up your tripod on a firm surface and spread the legs fully. Don't increase height by moving the legs closer together! For slippery or delicate surfaces, use a triangular *spreader* to distribute the weight.

The tripod dolly/rolling tripod
To allow a tripod to move around, you attach it to a castered base (*skid, skate*) when it becomes a *tripod dolly* or *rolling tripod*. (A flat smooth floor surface is essential to avoid picture judder). The dolly's wheels may move freely, or be *locked* to restrict their direction (for straight-line moves), and *wheel brakes* can be applied to immobilize dolly movement altogether.

Tripod
A simple three-legged stand, with independently extendable legs. Height cannot be adjusted during a shot. It can be set up on rough uneven ground. A spider (spreader) will prevent the feet from slipping, or sinking in soft ground.

Rolling tripod
A tripod on a castered base (skid/skate/rolling spider). The height is preset with a hand-crank (or pneumatic). Caster foot-brakes and cable-guards may be fitted. Easily wheeled on a flat smooth surface, steering may be erratic.

Lightweight pneumatic tripod (Hydro-Ped, PortaPed)
A robust tripod mounting, widely used in ENG/EFP production.

The Pedestal

A *pedestal* or *'ped'* is the workhorse of most larger studios. Basically, it is a central telescopic column of adjustable height, fixed to a three-wheeled base. Lightweight pedestals provide considerable shot flexibility, rapid height changes, and precision steering, even in confined spaces. The heaviest counterweighted types are cumbersome and limited by comparison.

Types of pedestal
Lightweight pneumatic tripods (*'PortaPed'*, *'Hydro-Ped'*) are widely used in the field, especially for ENG/EFP productions. In this portable design the pneumatically counterbalanced central column can be pumped up and down, and locked off at any height (e.g. 2 to 5 ft. (60 cms to 1·5 m)). Although normally used as a fixed tripod mounting, it can be fitted onto a *caster dolly (crabbing dolly)* three-wheeled base, to allow it to be moved around as a *pedestal*.

The standard *studio pedestal* has several design variations. Its telescopic central column may be controlled pneumatically, hydraulically, counterweighted, or hand-cranked.

Counterbalancing
Pedestals need vertical rebalancing whenever the weight of the camera and its accessories is changed – e.g. when a prompter is added or removed. (Small lead weights may be placed in a tray at the top of the column for fine adjustment.) When properly balanced, the camera height can be raised/lowered and left at any chosen height; secured perhaps, by a concentric *locking ring*. An incorrectly counterbalanced camera is liable to drift upwards/downwards, and be difficult to adjust.

Operating the pedestal
The pedestal's central column is normally fitted with a concentric *steering ring (steering wheel)* which is used both to steer the dolly around, and to raise and lower the camera. Some designs also have a handle or *tiller arm* to guide the dolly.

The pedestal's three rubber-tired wheels can be steered in :
• *Dolly (tricycle; tracking) mode* with single-wheel steering and two wheels' direction fixed. For general moves, and for dollying in curved tracks (*arcs*).
• *Crab (parallel) mode* with all three wheels interlinked to steer simultaneously. Used for sideways moves (*trucking; crabbing*) and moving into confined spaces.

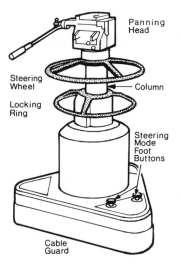

Panning Head

Steering Wheel

Locking Ring

Column

Steering Mode Foot Buttons

Cable Guard

The studio pedestal
A surround wheel or ring at the top of the column is used to adjust column height (hence the lens height) and to steer the pedestal. A second ring may be fitted to lock-off the column.

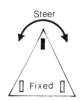

Pedestal steering
The pedestal's three rubber-tyred wheels may be linked together (foot pedal selection) for sideways moves in a *parallel* (*crab*) *mode*, or with single-wheel steering (two wheels fixed) in *dolly* (*tricycle*) *mode* for general dolly moves.

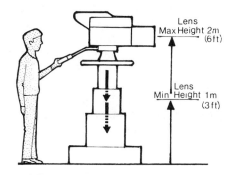

Lens Max Height 2m (6ft)

Lens Min Height 1m (3ft)

Lens height
Typical lens-height adjustments for a pedestal are from 2 m (6 ft) maximum to 1 m (3 ft) minimum.

37

Jibs and Cranes

As useful as the *pedestal* mounting is for everyday productions, there will always be situations where you need even greater flexibility. When you are shooting a dance sequence, a rock group, a drama production, or an orchestra for example, you often want:

• Greatly increased *camera heights* – positioning the camera some 10 ft. (3 m) or more above the action.

• Rapid *vertical movements* – which allow the camera to rise quickly and soar over the action; or to swoop down from a height; or to move in from a high distant viewpoint to join the performers.

Sideways movements – in which the camera gently repositions its viewpoint; or dramatically sweeps across as the action develops.

The *camera cranes* originally developed for film production provided this flexibility, and have been used successfully for many years in larger television studios. However, they had drawbacks. They can take up a lot of floor space and need unobstructed height to maneuver. They require a coordinated camera team of up to four people to operate and guide them. So several other types of mounting were developed for TV production.

The jib arm

This is a counter-balanced beam or *jib arm* supported on a pedestal, tripod, or wheeled base. At one end of this mounting, the remotely controlled lightweight/portable camera is hung in a cradle. The camera's controls are arranged at the other end of the jib arm, together with a picture monitor/viewfinder. With this arrangement, *one operator* can not only adjust pan, tilt, focus, and zoom while framing the shot to follow the action, but raise/lower the jib arm (*crane or boom* up/down), move the jib sideways (*tonguing* left/right), and move the entire dolly (*dollying/tracking* in and out; *trucking/crabbing* left/right). Further moves (*tongueing* the sideways jib in/out; *arcing* round a subject) are also possible.

How much any single operator can reasonably be expected to do, depends on the occasion! The jib arm is mainly used to provide a higher viewpoint from a stationary mounting (e.g. to about 10 ft. (3 m)), with occasional height changes in shot. Swinging the jib sideways is often much quicker, safer and more convenient than trucking the entire dolly.

Studio cranes

Small camera cranes are used, where the director requires both height variations (e.g. 1½ to 10 ft. (0·46 to 3 m)) and considerable mobility. Several forms of studio crane are available, from 'lightweight' collapsible mountings to giant cranes requiring experienced specialist operators.

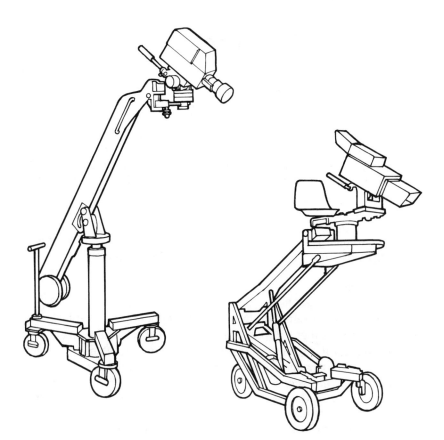

Jib arm

A counterbalanced beam mounted on a pedestal, tripod, or wheeled base. The video camera at its far end may be operated manually, or controlled remotely at its lower end, using an attached picture monitor.

Small crane

A lightweight crane (*Vinten*) for remotes and studio use. The height range (0.6 to 2m; 2 to 7 ft) with 360° seat and camera rotation, offer considerable shot flexibility.

Adjusting the Lens Aperture

As we saw earlier (Page 18), the lens system contains an adjustable *diaphragm* or *iris* formed from a series of flat interleaving metal blades. Turning an *iris control ring* at the near end of the lens barrel adjusts the size of this hole – the lens working aperture or *f-stop*.

The ring has a graduated scale with a series of standard *f-stop* settings. These relate to the proportion of the light passing through the lens system, and falling onto the pickup sensor (the *CCD*). You select a particular *f-stop* setting, by aligning it with an indicator mark.

The larger the maximum size of the lens aperture, the more light it will pass. When shooting under lower light levels, a camera using a *fast* lens (with a maximum aperture of e.g. *f*/1.5), will produce better pictures than one with a smaller maximum aperture of e.g. *f*/5.6 (a *slow* lens).

Adjusting the iris

There are several operational methods of adjusting the lens aperture:

• *Iris control ring* – Here you turn the *iris control ring* with the fingers of your left hand; the method widely used on portable video cameras.

• *Remote control* – Using this method, the *f-stop* is set to suit prevailing lighting conditions before shooting. Then as shots change, an operator at a remote *CCU* or *vision control console (base station)* varies the lens aperture slightly, to compensate for any unevenness in the lighting, or to enhance the artistic quality of the picture.

Studios are lit to a *standard light intensity*, and the equipment adjusted to suit this during a pre-rehearsal camera check (*camera set-up; line-up*).

• *Auto-iris* – An increasing number of cameras are provided with the option of an *auto-iris*, which self-adjusts the lens aperture to suit the scene brightness. We shall look at this facility more closely later, when considering automatic lens controls (Page 65).

The effect of adjustment

Adjusting the lens aperture has *two* important effects simultaneously:

1. It controls the brightness of the lens image reaching the CCD from the lens. So it affects the picture's *exposure* – i.e. the reproduced tonal values.

2. It will affect the depth zone within the scene (*depth of field*), in which subjects appear sharply focused.

In practical terms, as you will see, this means that you —

• Either adjust the lens aperture to expose the picture under prevailing lighting, and accept whatever depth of field results,

• Or select the *f-stop* that will provide the depth of field you require, and adjust the light intensity to give a correctly exposed picture (by adding illumination, or filtering the lens as appropriate).

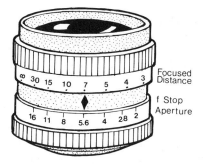

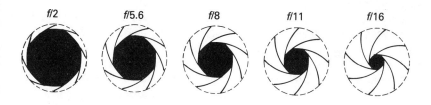

Adjustment

The lens aperture is adjusted by turning a ring on the lens barrel. The *f-stop* number opposite the marker shows the aperture selected. As the lens is stopped (irised) down, its aperture becomes smaller. (Light-transmission is reduced and depth of field increases.)

F-stops and transmission numbers

Lens apertures are often calibrated in a standard series of calculated markings such as: *f*/1.4, 2, 2.8, 4, 5.6, 8, 11, 16, 22. Transmission numbers indicate the amount of light passing through a lens system at various apertures, and can be taken as equivalent to corresponding *f*-stops.

Light transmission

The effect on the amount of light passing through the lens system, on changing to a new aperture, equals:

$$\frac{(\text{old } f\text{-number})^2}{(\text{new } f\text{-number})^2}$$

Thus from *f*/4 to *f*/8 the amount of light received by the camera tube is reduced by $4^2/8^2 = \frac{1}{4}$.

Light change

Opening a full stop increases the lens aperture to admit twice the original light e.g. *f*/8 to *f*/5.6. Opening half a stop increases the lens aperture to admit half as much light again as originally, e.g. *f*/8 to *f*/6.3.

Controlling Exposure

A picture is 'correctly exposed' when the tones you are most interested in are clearly reproduced.

Light levels

The camera needs a certain amount of light from the scene to produce pictures with good tonal gradation, color fidelity, and little picture noise.

If it receives *too little light* – because of insufficient illumination, or the lens aperture being too small (*stopped down*), the picture becomes *under-exposed*. All tones appear unduly dark, shadows merge lifelessly, picture noise speckles darker tones, and spurious effects develop (e.g. lag, shading). You can't compensate for bad under-exposure by increasing *video gain*. It just makes the picture brighter, and defects more noticeable.

When the CCD receives *too much light*, surface tones look paler than normal. Light areas *block-off* to a detailless white. Color looks *'washed-out'* (*desaturated*) – although shadow details become clearer. Reduced video gain will not compensate for initial *over-exposure*.

Basic solutions

Under-exposure – Open up the lens aperture, or increase the illumination. Will re-positioning the camera to suit the existing light help? Where your subject is clear enough but the overall picture lacks 'bite', increasing the video gain can improve matters considerably.

Over-exposure – You can do the reverse. Keep tonal extremes (e.g. sky) out of shot. You might modify an overbright subject (e.g. use a darker table cover). Where *stopping down* increases the depth of field noticeably, use a neutral-density lens filter to reduce the overall image brightness.

Tonal contrast

Everyday scenes often contain very strong tonal contrasts, where the lightest tones are 160 times as bright as the darkest (160:1). That is not surprising, for a surface's brightness depends not only on tone and texture, but on its angle to the light, and the amount of light falling upon it.

Although our eyes can clearly discern intermediate tonal differences throughout a range of 100:1 your camera can only reproduce a relatively limited tonal range with reasonable accuracy. Beyond that range, the original tones will appear crushed out to white or black in the picture.

While *camera tubes* accommodate a 20:1 to 30:1 range, *CCD sensors* can handle 40:1 contrasts. However, *TV receivers* typically reproduce a 20:1 range or less, so subtle gradations in a multi-toned scene may be lost, particularly in highlights and shadows.

Selective exposure

The video camera's great advantage, is that you can judge 'correct exposure' immediately from the viewfinder or monitor picture, and adjust the lens aperture (*f-stop*) for the best results. Although some cameras have a viewfinder indicator that draws your attention to over-exposed areas, the best exposure setting must always be an artistic choice. In most scenes, *the appearance of faces* is your main guide to adjusting exposure. Unless you are aiming at dramatic effects, the performer's features should look well-modeled and neither abnormally light nor dark. Having exposed faces effectively, you may have to accept that the reproduction of extreme tones in the rest of the shot is a compromise. Shadows may appear detailless, and the lightest tones merge. (Perhaps lighting can be modified to improve the situation.)

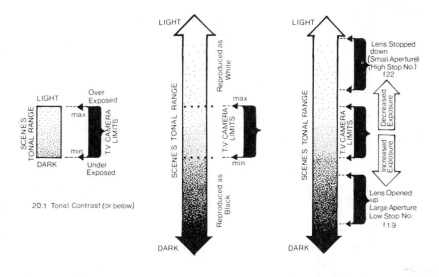

Controlling the exposure

The camera tube can reproduce only a relatively limited tonal range accurately. If scenic tones exceed the camera tube's limits, detail and tonal gradation in the lightest and darkest tones are crushed out.

As you adjust the lens aperature (*f*-stop), the narrow tonal range accepted by the camera moves up/down the scenic tonal scale, selecting which part is to be reproduced successfully.

Opening up the aperture progressively improves shadow detail, but increasingly over-exposes light tones.

Stopping down progressively improves clarity in lightest tones, but darker tones merge.

43

Focusing — The Principles

Strictly speaking, a lens only gives an absolutely sharp image for subjects at the distance to which it is focused (the *focused plane*). In practice however, things that are nearer or further away may still look reasonably sharp. The depth of this 'sharpness zone', can vary considerably; from a few centimeters to *infinity* (α)! Outside this zone, which is called the *depth of field*, subjects appear increasingly soft-focused.

What affects the depth of field?
The depth of field changes whenever you alter –
- The *focused distance* – i.e. how far away you are focused.
- The lens's *focal length* – i.e. the *zoom* setting (hence the *lens angle*).
- The lens *aperture* – i.e. the *f-stop* you are working at.

Change *any* of these, and this sharpness zone gets deeper *or* shallower!

Does this effect really matter?
In a long shot, the focused zone can be considerable; But take a big closeup of something nearby, and you may not be able to get the entire subject in focus! When a subject is textured or patterned, this fall off in sharpness will be very obvious; but where surfaces are plain, some defocusing is not always obvious.

Depth of field can become quite shallow when you use the zoom lens set to a *long focal length (long focus lens; narrow lens angle)* – i.e. when 'zoomed right in', particularly with a *large lens aperture* (*a large stop; e.g. f/1.9*). Accurate focusing may be difficult, especially when shooting close-ups.

Use the same zoom lens set to a *short focal length (wide lens angle)* – i.e. 'zoomed right out', and particularly when it has a *small lens aperture* (*stopped right down; e.g. f/16*), everything in the picture will look sharp.

Following focus
As the camera moves, or the subject distance changes, you may need to re-adjust focus. Whether focusing is critical or not depends on the depth of field available and the detail visible. In a close-up, even slight subject movement may necessitate refocusing. In a longer shot, quite widespread movements may still remain within the focused zone.

Many narrow-angle/long-focus lenses (e.g. of 5° or less) cannot focus sharply on anything closer than a meter or so away (its *minimum focusing distance – MFD*). For extremely close shots, you will need to use the zoom lens' *macro setting*, or fit a *positive supplementary lens* attachment.

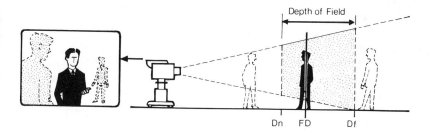

Types of focus control
1. Spoked capstan knob.   2. Twist grip.   3. Camera focus handle.

Depth of field
Within the *depth of field* a lens subjects appear sharp, although maximum sharpness occurs at the focused distance (focused plane), FD. Outside this zone (nearer than Dn or further away than Df) sharpness falls off rapidly and subjects become defocused.

Focusing — The Problems

Except for the odd occasion where you deliberately *de*focus for effect (e.g. to suggest dizziness), you normally try to keep your main subject focused as sharply as possible. Anyone can tell whether a printed page is in focus, but you will meet situations where focusing is much less exact. When shooting *faces*, use the eyes (sometimes the teeth or hair) to judge. If necessary, rock the focus control to and fro to get the sharpest image. In longer shots, use *costume detail* for focus checks. Take care that you don't inadvertently focus on prominent *background detail*, while your less defined *main subject* remains 'soft'! It happens!

Selective focusing

In most situations, we adjust the lens aperture to correct the exposure: *stopping down* in bright light; *opening up* under dim conditions. We accept whatever depth of field results. But there are times when you want to select the *f-stop* to present the subject in a particular way:

• *Deep-focus techniques* – Here the aim is to show everything in the scene from close foreground to the furthest distance, sharply focused. That may be ideal when shooting widespread action, or where several subjects are at different distances from the camera. But continual overall clarity can lead to pictures that look flat, and lack atmosphere, unless the lighting is dramatic, with strong perspective.

For maximum depth, the lens must be stopped down – and that will necessitate considerable light levels. An alternative is to focus the lens at the *hyperfocal distance*.

• *Shallow-focus techniques* – To isolate close subjects against a blurred background, use a large lens aperture to restrict focused depth. In this way you can separate a foreground speaker from distracting or confusing background action, or prevent a flower from merging with its leafy surroundings. To avoid over-exposure, use a *neutral density (ND)* filter.

Shifting focus

When you have insufficient depth of field, yet cannot stop down:

• You can *pull-focus* – But in a static shot, the effect of throwing focus between subjects at different distances can become over-dramatic.

• Try *splitting focus* – Adjust for the best overall focus compromise; even if this means that nothing is really sharp.

• Take a *wider shot (longer shot)* – Zooming out a little will increase the depth of field to some extent. But remember, if you widen the shot to improve focusing, and then dolly in until the image size is the same as originally, you will land up with the same depth of field as you started with!

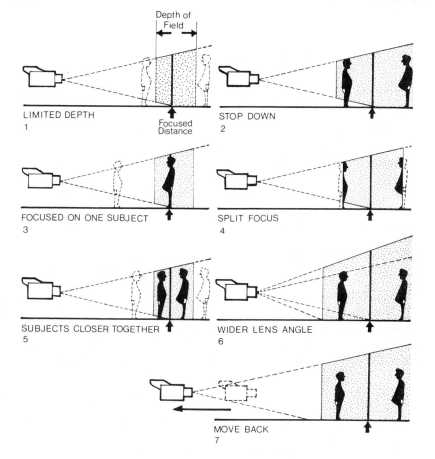

LIMITED DEPTH
1

Depth of Field

Focused Distance

STOP DOWN
2

FOCUSED ON ONE SUBJECT
3

SPLIT FOCUS
4

SUBJECTS CLOSER TOGETHER
5

WIDER LENS ANGLE
6

MOVE BACK
7

Limited depth of field – solving the problem

1. Depth of field may be too restricted to focus more than one subject properly.
2. *Stop down* – focused depth increases but exposure is reduced.
3. *Focus on one subject* – allow others to become unsharp.
4. *Split focus* – depth of field is spread between both subjects, making them equally unsharp.
5. *Move subject* – place both subjects at roughly the same distance from the camera.
6. *Use wider lens angle (zoom out)* – depth of field increases but subjects now look smaller.
7. *Pull camera further away* – depth increases but subject appears further away.

Hyperfocal distance

If a lens is adjusted to its *hyperfocal distance*, everything from half this distance to infinity is reasonably sharp. To find the hyperfocal distance (H):

$$H_{ft} = \frac{(\text{focal length of lens in inches})^2}{\text{lens stop no.} \times 0.002}$$

$$H_m = \frac{(\text{focal length in cm})^2 \times 100}{\text{lens stop no.} \times 0.05}$$

47

Depth of Field in Practice

While you are shooting and concentrating on the action, the available depth of field can vary without your realizing it. So be prepared! Remember, when you refocus as the *distance* of the subject or camera alters, or you operate the *zoom*, or you change the *f-stop* (e.g. opening it up as you move into a building), the depth of field will alter! You will notice this most on closer shots.

As a rough guide, about *one-third* of the focused depth extends in front of the focused distance (*focused plane*) and *two-thirds* beyond it. The overall depth available at a given stop is greater for smaller CCD formats.

Adjusting light intensity

Most lenses perform best when they are only *partially* stopped down (e.g. f/5·6 to f/8). Although the obvious answer to restricted depth of field is to stop the lens right down (e.g. to f/16), this is usually impracticable under typical light levels, and can lead to inferior picture quality.

You can light some subjects (e.g. machinery, statues or coins), to very high intensities to ensure maximum depth of field. But others such as plants, delicate materials, and people, may be harmed under such dazzlingly hot conditions. Ventilation too can become a problem.

If you open up a lens to *maximum aperture* in order to reduce focused depth or when shooting under low-light conditions, picture definition and tonal clarity may deteriorate as optical defects become obvious (flare, aberrations).

ND filters are obtainable in a series of densities, to aid exposure control. But lower quality filters are liable to degrade clarity to some extent.

Practical operation

Zooming in, depth of field decreases. *Zooming out,* the reverse happens. When someone walks to or from the camera, the zoom's *focal length* will influence how much you have to readjust the focus control to compensate for their changing distance and how critical focusing becomes.

You soon become aware of how shallow the depth of field really can be when working with a *long focal length* lens (*zoomed in; telephoto; narrow angle*). If you are moving around and then suddenly zoom in, focusing can be quite hazardous!

Focusing is easiest when using a *short focal length* lens (*zoomed out; wide angle*). Thanks to the greater depth of field, focusing may hardly need adjustment. But of course, everything now looks so far away! And as we shall see, moving closer can produce noticeable distortions.

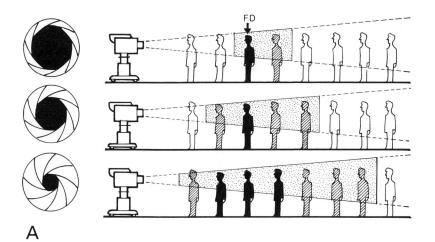

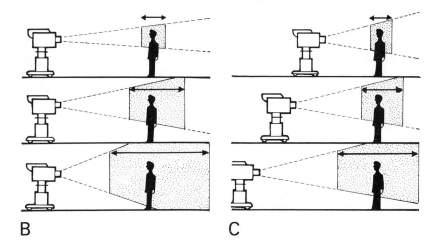

When depth of field changes

A. *Lens aperture.* As the lens is stopped down, depth of field increases.

B. *Lens angle.* As the lens angle increases (shorter focal length), depth of field increases.

C. *Camera distance.* The further away the camera focuses, the greater the depth of field.

Focal Length and Lens Angle

Two important pieces of information are marked at the front of a zoom lens: its maximum and minimum *focal lengths* (in inches or millimeters), and its maximum *aperture* or *f-stop*.

Altering the focal length

If you change the lens's focal length by altering the zoom lens setting, the subject will look correspondingly larger or smaller in the picture; and the impression of distance can alter. *Double* the focal length and your subject appears twice as large (apparently closer) – but only half the previous height and width of the scene is visible. At the same time, depth appears squashed.

If instead you *halve* the focal length, the subject is shown half the original size (apparently further away). The shot shows twice as much of the scene height and width than before. Depth appears exaggerated.

Lens angle

For convenience, people often refer to '*using a two-inch lens*' for a scene. But you cannot accurately estimate a lens's coverage, or the size and proportions that subjects will have from the *focal length* alone. For that, you need to know the *lens angles*. These you can work out from the *focal length* setting, *and* the size of the light sensor.

The camera lens show us a *rectangular* wedge of the scene in four by three proportions – i.e. an *aspect ratio* of 4:3 or 1.33:1. If it covers a *horizontal angle* of 40° for example (from left to right frame-edge), its *vertical* angle (from top to bottom frame) will be 30°.

The real advantage of thinking in terms of *lens angles*, rather than *focal lengths*, is that shot detail is completely predictable for *any* lens, with any size CCD or light sensor. If you draw the *horizontal lens angle* on a plan to any scale, it immediately reveals:

- The shots available from any camera position.
- The relative sizes of everything in the picture.
- Exactly what will appear in the shot, and what is lost outside the frame.
- The effect of changing the lens angle (i.e. zooming in or out).

As before, change the lens angle and the subject size will alter correspondingly.

Similarly, you can use the *vertical lens angle* (which is three-quarters of the horizontal angle) to check against scale *elevations* (side-views) of the scene, and see whether there is any danger of your shooting too high (*overshooting*).

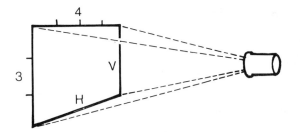

Angle of view
The video camera's lens sees in 4:3 proportions. So its vertical angle of view is three-quarters of its horizontal angle. The longer the focal length, the narrower the lens angle.

Camera formats compared
Image sensor size: 18mm (⅔in)
Image format: 8.8×6.6mm (0.35×0.26in)
'Normal' lens focal length about 11mm (0.4in)

| Focal length | | Lens angle | |
mm	in	Horizontal	Vertical
6.0	0.24	72.5°	57.5°
9.0	0.35	52.0°	40.0°
10.0	0.39	47.5°	35.5°
12.5	0.5	38.5°	29.5°
25.0	1.0	19.0°	14.5°
55.0	2.0	9.0°	7.0°
110.0	4.3	4.5°	3.5°
235.0	9.3	2.0°	1.5°
550.0	17.7	1.0°	0.75°

Camera tube size: 25mm (1in)
Image format: 12.8×9.6mm (12.8×9.6in)
'Normal' lens focal length about 16–20mm (0.6–0.8in)

| Focal length | | Lens angle | |
mm	in	Horizontal	Vertical
12.5	0.5	54.0°	40.0°
25.0	1.0	27.0°	20.0°
50.0	2.0	13.5°	10.0°
75.0	3.0	9.0°	7.0°
150.0	6.0	4.5°	3.5°

Varying the Lens Angle

In a well-balanced sequence, there are wider shots (*long shots*) showing the broad action and its location; and closer shots (*close-ups, mid-shots*) concentrating attention on particular features. Each type of shot has its part to play in persuading and holding the audience's interest.

Moving the camera

The most obvious method of adjusting shots is to change the position of your camera. For *closer shots* you simply move nearer; the subject itself appears larger and surroundings are gradually excluded. Moving further away for a *longer shot*, the subject now appears smaller, and you reveal more of the surroundings. You could shoot an entire production very successfully with the zoom lens left at around 25°. This straightforward approach does have its disadvantages however:

• To vary shot sizes you would have to continually move the camera. That can be time-consuming and tiring.

• When recording continuously, this can produce a lot of irrelevant material, that has to be edited out. If you stop recording while you move the camera, you may miss some of the action.

• Alternatively, you may be able to *stop the action* while moving the camera. But then it will be necessary to have the performer/talent repeat the end of previous action, to provide overlaps for editing.

• Frequent camera moves to vary the shot size can look very fidgety.

• When intercutting between several cameras shooting the same subject, there is always the danger that one camera will come into another's shot.

A range of angles available

Changing to a different focal length, does two fundamental things:

• It varies the apparent nearness, prominence, importance of the subject.

• It decides how much of the action and the surroundings your audience is aware of, and can see. Unless they have previous knowledge of what is going on (or can hear clues), they will not know what they are missing out of shot (e.g. an onlooking crowd).

Within the range of a 15:1 zoom lens, you can fill the screen with a wide overall view of a street (e.g. 50°) or a poster that was previously scarcely visible (e.g. 5°) – all without moving the camera. So clearly, you could avoid moving the camera altogether, simply by readjusting the lens to alter the shot size. Many people do just that! But as you will see, that can produce some very undesirable side-effects. Where possible, it is much more effective to move your camera around on a *normal* lens angle, only varying its focal length when there is some practical advantage.

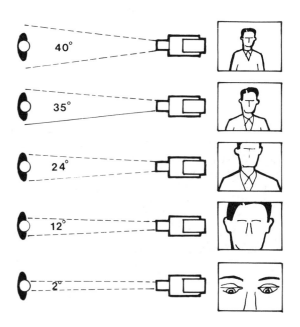

Coverage changes
How much of the scene is covered by the lens (its angle of view) depends on its focal length, relative to the camera tube's image size. As the len's focal length is changed, its angle of view alters correspondingly. For example, if you use a lens of one-third the focal length, the angle of view becomes three times as wide. Three times as much of the scene is covered but subjects appear a third of their previous size in the shot.

Lens Angle and Perspective

If the angle of your camera lens is similar to the angle at which the viewers are watching their TV screens (e.g. 20° – 25°), then the perspective in their pictures will look accurate. Sizes and distances seem natural.

When you use a much wider lens angle (*shorter focal length*) or narrower lens angle (*longer focal length*), the apparent depth and scale on the screen will differ from those in the original scene.

Forms of distortion

The narrow-angle lens – As the lens angle *narrows* not only do things look closer, but the screen shows a smaller and smaller segment of the scene. As a result, pictorial perspective appears *flattened*. Depth seems *compressed*. The foreground-to-background distance is reduced, and subjects that are far away appear disproportionately large. Distant people and buildings may look like cut-outs. Anything moving to or from the camera seems to cover the distance very slowly. Camera *dollying* (*tracking*) looks remarkably slow, and produces only gradual visual changes.

The wide-angle lens – As you *widen* the lens angle, perspective becomes increasingly *exaggerated*. Space, depth and distance are *emphasized*, looking far greater than they really are. Even subjects that are not all that far away, seem unnaturally small. People appear to cover the ground in rapid strides as they approach. Dollying seems much faster than normal.

Deliberate distortion

Theoretically these various distortions arise whenever the lens angle varies from 'normal', but they only start to become really noticeable below about 10° and above 30°. They are most obvious in scenes with strong perspective clues, such as architectural subjects, repeated patterns, railway tracks, etc. Perspective distortion is least apparent where there are few visual clues, as in shots of open spaces.

You can use perspective distortion to create *deliberate* spatial effects:

The narrow-angle lens – You can reduce the impression of depth and space; create a compressed 'crowded-in' effect; group together distant and nearby subjects – e.g. pulling together a straggling parade that stretches away into the distance.

The wide-angle lens – Even cramped confined spaces can be made to look much bigger on the screen when shot with a wide-angle lens. A modestly sized setting can seem spacious. You can also use the wide-angle lens dramatically – e.g. to emphasize gestures in low-angle shots, or to distort subjects in close-ups.

Viewing distance

The distance from which you watch a TV picture should vary with the size of the screen. Too close and no extra subject detail is visible. Too far from it and you cannot see all available detail. To see maximum detail, a distance of 4–6 times picture height is often recommened. The screen is at an angle of about 20°–27° to the eye. When the camera lens horizontal angle is roughly similar, perspective in the picture appears natural.

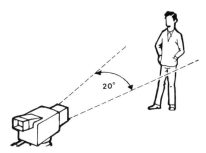

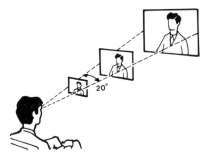

Natural perspective

If you watch the screen from too far away, or a wide-angle lens is used to shoot the scene, depth and distance appear exaggerated in the picture. Viewed too closely,or shot with a narrow lens angle, depth and distance are compressed and distant subjects look unnaturally large.

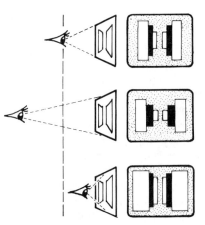

Why Change The Lens Angle?

Although most video cameras are fitted with a zoom lens, we only use the zooming action occasionally. More often, we select a particular *angle* or *focal length* within its range, and shoot at that setting.

Our impressions of distance, scale and proportion can be distorted whenever the camera's lens angle differs from normal, but there are many practical advantages in having a *selection* of lens angles available. They can greatly extend shot opportunities.

How changing the lens angle can help
• *Adjusting framing without moving the camera –*
To provide a variety of shot sizes.
Slightly widening or narrowing the shot to improve the picture's balance.
To correct framing (e.g. when people move off marked positions).
Adjusting to exclude/include other subjects, or nearby distractions.
To precisely frame a subject (e.g. a map or graphic).
• *Providing shots that would otherwise be impracticable –*
Narrow angles for close shots of distant or inaccessible subjects when:
    The camera is isolated (e.g. on a rooftop)
    There are obstructions (uneven ground) preventing movement.
    The subject is inaccessible (e.g. beyond water; behind bars).
    You are using a fixed tripod.
Wide angles giving you a broader view of the scene when:
    Space is limited.
    There is no room to move the camera back from the subject.
• *Altering the apparent subject distance quickly –*
Where there is insufficient time to move the camera.
During fast intercutting, where rapid camera moves may be impracticable, or may involve complicated dolly moves.
• *Avoiding camera movement –*
Where this would distract performer/talent, or obscure action from the audience or other cameras.
• *Simplifying camerawork –*
Zooming can be smoother, faster, more accurate than dollying; particularly on flat subjects, where the effect is the same.
• *Deliberately adjusting apparent perspective or proportions in the shot –*
Using a wider lens angle to exaggerate space; or a narrower angle to compress it.
Increasing the lens angle and reducing the camera distance (or vice versa) to alter the foreground/background proportions.

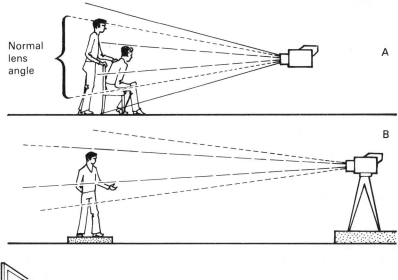

Normal lens angle

A

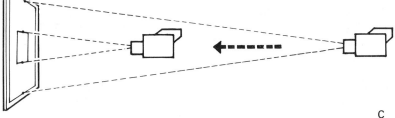

B

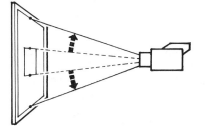

C

Typical problems

A. When there is insufficient time to dolly, or if movement would distract the performers or hide them from a nearby audience, widen/narrow the lens angle instead.

B. If the camera is fixed or uneven ground prevents it moving, change the lens angle.

C. When a camera dollies in to detail, there can be focusing, framing and movement problems. If the camera zooms instead, these difficulties do not occur.

Lens Angle Problems

There are really two ways in which you can organize shooting:
• Choose a camera position, then adjust the zoom lens' focal length until you get the shot you want. But that is liable to result in haphazard mixtures of perspective (proportion and distance) in the course of a scene.
• Set the zoom lens to a 'normal' angle of around 20°– 25°, then move the camera to a position where you have the right length of shot.

The normal lens

A *normal* lens angle gives few problems. The viewfinder's perspective looks similar to that of the scene in front of you. The 'feel' of the camera seems natural – the way it handles, focuses, frames.

When shooting in small rooms though, a *normal* lens may not give you sufficient coverage. (You might try shooting through a doorway or window.) In cramped surroundings, it is often better to use a *wider* lens angle; although this will make the room seem larger. Where a foreground area looks empty and uninteresting on a normal lens, the effect can often be improved by *reducing* the lens angle.

The narrow-angle lens

Using a narrow-angle lens, a camera can be difficult to control smoothly. It is hard to avoid jerky movements, and to keep the subject accurately framed. Below about 5° a firm mounting is essential. It may even be necessary to *lock the panning head* to prevent camera shake or wind rock.

Because depth of field becomes shallower as the angle narrows (zooming in), accurate focusing becomes more difficult. The focus control may feel very coarse, so that even slight re-adjustments throw the entire subject out of focus. Subjects moving towards or away from the camera easily pass beyond the focused zone, particularly in closer shots.

Heat haze can produce an overall shimmering in close shots of distant subjects. The only solution is to move nearer. The characteristic depth-squashing that narrow-angle lenses produce on close-ups can only be overcome by widening the lens angle and moving closer.

The wide-angle lens

Although popular for their greater depth of field and easy handling, wide-angle lenses cause subjects to appear too small and distant, and foreground space often looks excessive.

Close shots show considerable distortion, particularly on movements towards the camera. And because the camera is so near the subject, it is liable to cast shadows onto it, making lighting difficult. Wide-angle lenses are more susceptible to *lens flares* (especially in long shots), from any illumination pointing towards the camera (*backlight*).

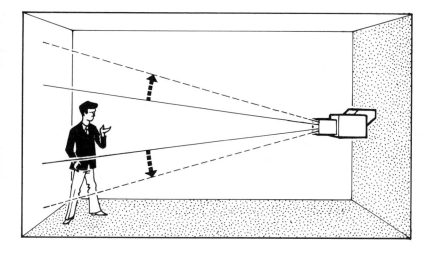

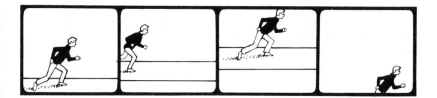

Limited room
If the camera cannot move far enough away to get sufficient coverage on a normal-angle lens, widening the lens angle can help.

Varying framing
When following a moving subject with a narrow-angle (long-focus) lens, you are liable to produce an uneven weaving shot. Constant framing is extremely difficult.

The Zoom Lens

Zoom lenses vary considerably in design and optical quality. As you would expect, precision systems are correspondingly more expensive, and are generally much larger.

Lens limitations

Whether any lens's limitations are apparent, will largely depend on the kind of subjects you are shooting. Where your audience is concentrating on the action (e.g. newscasts), or the subjects themselves are less critical (e.g. general location shots), any shortcomings will usually be overlooked anyway. But there are situations where any defects will be obvious to even the casual viewer.

If for instance, you take close shots of graph paper, sheet music, maps or fine print, and slowly zoom in and out, you may well find that:

• The image is not as sharp as you would have liked. The *resolution* (*definition*) is too limited.

• Sharpness drifts as the focal length is altered, and the *focus* control needs to be readjusted to compensate (*tracking error*).

• The picture's brightness or *exposure* varies as the focal length is changed (varying *light transmission*). This may only happen at the telephoto end of the zoom range (*ramping*).

• Distortions develop, especially at the corners and edges of the frame. Straight lines bend, areas stretch or contract (*geometrical distortion*).

• Various optical shortcomings (*aberrations*) may soften the image, producing *flare* (*veiling*), unevenness (*shading*), etc. *Internal reflections* can cause ghost images of e.g. oncoming cars' headlamps and street lights.

Zoom lens design

Zoom lenses are made with maximum/minimum angle ratios ranging from 5:1 to 40:1 or more. Many introduce a flip-in *extender lens* in mid-range (with some overlap) to increase the overall coverage – but at the expense of reduced definition and light losses.

The shot box

Studio cameras are often fitted with a *shot box*. It may be attached to a panning handle, or integrated into the camera head itself. This device has push-buttons which select *pre-set lens angles*. You can switch instantly or at an adjustable speed, to pre-arranged shot sizes. Otherwise you have to rely on your memory, and adjust the zoom while watching the viewfinder, or check the settings on a built-in meter. Where a director has planned to use certain lens angles for pre-arranged camera positions, you can set up the shot box to these chosen angles.

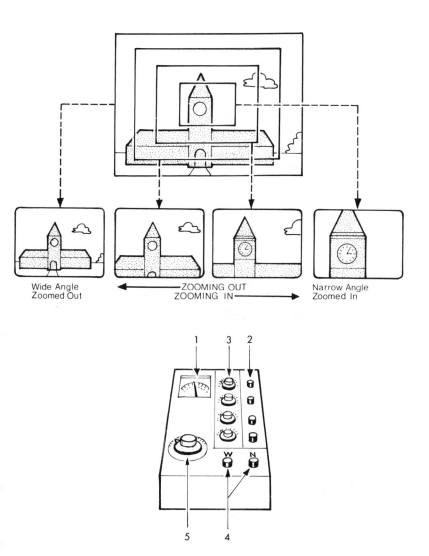

Wide Angle
Zoomed Out

◄─── ZOOMING OUT
ZOOMING IN ───►

Narrow Angle
Zoomed In

Zooming
Zooming-in progressively fills the screen with a smaller section of the scene (narrowing the lens angle; increasing the focal length).

Shot-box
Located on a pan-bar or in the camera head, the shot-box pre-selects lens angles.
(1) Meter indicates focal length/lens angle; (2) angle-select buttons; (3) pre-set angle for button selection; (4) move to widest/narrowest angle; (5) zoom speed.

Zoom Lens Problems

At first sight, using a zoom lens is simplicity itself, for all you have to do is to adjust it until you have the right shot, then focus up. But there is much more to it than that! A zoom lens behaves differently throughout its range.

Take care!
Long focal length / narrow-angle setting —
As we saw earlier, when the zoom lens is 'zoomed in' towards its *telephoto* limit it has certain frustrating features:
- It is difficult to hold the shot still (camera shake, unsteady framing).
- Depth of field can be shallow; subjects easily move out of the focused zone.
- Focusing can be very critical; it may be hard to judge what *is* in focus.
- Slight focus control adjustments can produce considerable changes.
- Perspective appears compressed.

Short focal length / wide-angle setting —
When zoomed out towards the *wide-angle* (W) limit, the problems change:
- Depth is so great, that everything seems equally sharp.
- It can be difficult to see exactly where the *focused plane* is located in the shot.
- Perspective is exaggerated.
- Picture defects such as lens flares and geometrical distortions can arise.
- Handling is much easier on a wide-angle setting, but the speeds of camera movements tend to be emphasized.

Pre-focusing the zoom lens
Have you ever taken a correctly focused shot on a *wide-angle* setting . . . then zoomed in to a detail in the scene . . . only to find that the new subject is *completely out of focus*? This happens all too easily.

In a wide shot, focusing is much broader thanks to the greater depth of field. (And in many viewfinders you may not be able to judge *where* you are sharply focused.) When you zoom in, the depth of field becomes restricted, and focusing extremely critical. Unless the lens was accurately focused on that subject, any error will be all too obvious in the close-up.

Wherever possible therefore, try to anticipate any zoom-in by sneaking a *pre-focus check* beforehand. Zoom in . . . focus hard on the close-up . . . then zoom out again to the current wide shot. When the moment comes to zoom, you know that the subject will remain quite sharp. Otherwise you might find yourself making a dramatic zoom in . . . to a fuzzy picture, which you have to refocus on-air, or reshoot.

The need to pre-focus

In a wide-angle shot, considerable depth of field makes it difficult to see exactly where the lens is focused most sharply.

At the lens angle narrows, depth of field becomes more restricted. So when zooming-in you may find that the focused plane is not at the subject, and it is out of focus in the close-up.

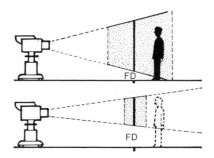

Changing perspective

Zooming-in on a three-dimensional scene causes changes in apparent perspective and proportions. Distance and depth become accentuated at wide angles but flattened and compressed as the lens angle narrows.

Zooming-in on a *flat* surface results only in a change in magnification. Proportions do not alter.

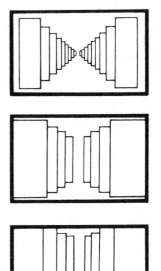

63

Automatic Controls

Most cameras can be operated either –
• By adjusting various controls *manually* to suit shooting conditions,
• Or relying on the camera's *automatic controls* to make corrections.
Each method has its advantages and drawbacks, and you learn with experience which is most likely to produce the best results at any time. In most cases, you can choose whichever technique is preferable.

Types of auto-control
There are several systems and design variants. When working under difficult conditions, they can be more reliable than a human operator. At worst, they can even prevent you from taking the shots you want!
    Typical automatic camera controls include:

Motorized zoom	Auto-focus
Auto-exposure	Automatic gain control (*AGC*)
Automatic white balance	Automatic black balance
Automatic gamma	Automatic image stabilizer

Motorized zoom
Instead of operating the zoom control by hand, you can press a switch, and have the lens zoom in/out automatically. The speed of the zoom motor varies with the pressure you put on a rocker switch, or the setting of a pre-set *zoom rate* control. The result is a smooth even action, that may be difficult to achieve by hand. However, *manual* zooming allows you to make subtle corrections in framing; e.g. expanding/contracting the coverage of a group shot as people enter and exit from it. When zooming manually to follow movement, it is much easier to compensate for the unexpected, than when using a motorized zoom.

Auto-focus
I.R. systems – The camera sends a small beam of infra-red light, which reflects from the subject onto a sensor. The time taken to travel is measured, and interpreted as the subject distance. This system's reaction time is slow (1·5 to 3 secs), but it works well in low light conditions. However, its range is limited, and the subject must be center frame. Due to false reflections, it is unreliable for subjects beyond glass, water, etc.

    Piezo systems – A reflected signal from a tiny piezo-electric element controls a motor which re-adjusts the lens for the sharpest picture signal. On the viewfinder screen, a series of rectangles show which part of the shot you have selected to focus on. A rapid system, least confused by difficult subjects, it can focus accurately down to extremely short distances.

Digital A.I. systems – Here a vibrating piezo element within the lens adjusts focus, controlled by *artificial intelligence* circuits.

Auto-tracking systems – Another piezo system, which locks onto the subject, maintaining focus wherever it moves within the frame.

Contrast control system – Focusing self-adjusts until subjects within a selected zone of the viewfinder are focused for maximum brightness and contrast. *Fuzzy logic* systems search beyond this zone where necessary to find and sharpen a nearly-focused area.

Problem subjects

Different auto-focus systems can be fooled by certain situations:
- Subjects behind glass, foliage, bars/netting, fences, etc.
- Smooth highly reflective subjects (glossy, curved, metallic).
- Low contrast subjects (plain-toned).
- Very dark subjects (light absorbent).
- Certain patterns (stripes – slanting or horizontal).
- When using various lens filters for special effects.
- Fast moving subjects.
- Weather conditions (e.g. rain, snow, fog).
- Dim lighting.

Auto-exposure control (auto-iris)

The design of this control varies between camera systems. Basically, it reads the brightness of the lens's image falling onto the CCD, and re-sets the iris to keep it constant, so preventing over-exposure. Some auto-irises set both the lens aperture *and* the *shutter speed* when adjusting exposure. Some allow you to select a subject, then *exposure-lock* on it.

Most systems are mainly controlled by center-frame tones, but others have an upper-frame bias, to prevent bright skies from falsely reducing the exposure. Others assess all picture tones when adjusting exposure.

When shooting subjects against a bright background (e.g. sky), a *backlight compensator* can be switched in to avoid the iris closing excessively and producing a silhouette. This device opens the iris a little, but leaves the auto-iris circuitry in operation.

The main limitation of automatic exposure control systems, is that they can operate 'irrationally', changing whenever the picture-content alters. If you pan or zoom to include a lighter or darker area, the exposure changes for the *entire picture* including your main subject, which ideally should remain constant. As the iris fluctuates, face and background tones vary; depth of field changes.

Auto-iris has major advantages if you are moving around rapidly from sunny exteriors to shadowy interiors. It can compensate (however arbitrarily) for extreme changes in light level, producing very acceptable pictures where continual manual readjustments would be quite empirical!

Classifying Shots

Your camera does so much more than just 'take a picture' of a situation. It gives your audience a certain impression of the subject and its surroundings. It concentrates their attention, or allows it to drift over a scene to settle on whatever catches their interest.

Shoot a subject one way and it can appear important, dominating its environment. Shot from another angle, the same subject often becomes quite incidental. It may even be overlooked. So we need a general method of classifying shots, to help us organize and arrange how we are going to shoot any situation.

It might be argued that because the TV screen is relatively small, the closer the viewpoint, the more effective the shot is; but even very broad panoramic or spectacular situations can still have considerable audience impact, as we see daily on our TV screens. Although cinema screens are large, their effective size is often surprisingly comparable.

Defining the shot

How we define any shot, usually depends on *how much of the screen is filled by the subject*. How you get that *shot size* is not relevant to classification. You can for example, get an identically sized close-up by using a wide-angle lens close to the subject, or a more distant camera with a narrow-angle lens. But the *overall effect* will be very different between these choices, for the picture's perspective and proportions change with the *focal length/lens angle* you are using.

General classifications

Even where a picture does not include people, we need quick convenient ways of indicating the shot's coverage.

• *Very long shots (vista shots)* – Here people occupy only a small proportion of the screen and may even be quite incidental to the shot. Emphasis is on broad views; on space and distance. You can introduce such shots to establish location (e.g. a seashore), or to reveal how one action group relates to another (e.g. in an arena full of dance groups).

• *Long shots (full shot)* – These provide distant views showing general details of subject(s), together with their immediate surroundings. A long shot of people around a table, would be sufficiently close for us to see their gestures and expressions, yet distant enough for us to appreciate the decor of the room. Long shots help us to build up an atmospheric effect, to convey a general mood, and follow fast or wide-ranging action.

• *Close shots* – Used broadly to refer to a complete object, or just a small part of it, the emphasis here is on *detail*. Obviously, a 'close shot' of an elephant's head and a closeup of a coin are very different propositions, but in practice, this all-purpose term is surprisingly useful.

Shot size

You can get the same kind of shot from a close position using a wide-angle lens, or from a more distant position with a narrower angle. Depth of field remains identical for the same size shot, although perspective appears different.

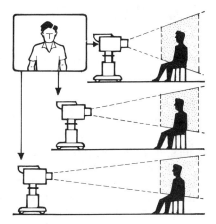

General classifications

Broad terms are often sufficient to indicate the sort of shot required.

(a) A long shot/full shot shows overall action in a distant view.

(b) A wide shot/cover shot shows performers and their surroundings in broad detail.

(c) A very long shot/vista shot reveals general location.

(d) A close shot/tight shot concentrates on detail.

(a)

(b)

(c)

(d)

67

Basic Shots of People

Does it really matter how you compose pictures of people? Isn't it just a matter of convention to classify the various ways in which you can shoot a person?

Over the years, a series of universally agreed 'standard shots' evolved in film-making. These were not simply routines, but compositions that experience has shown provide the most successful, artistically pleasing results. If you frame people in any other way, you will usually find that the effect looks awkward and unbalanced.

These easily recognized shots of people provide convenient quick reference points for all members of the production team; particularly the director and camera operator.

General terms
First of all, there are the broad directions used when describing shots –
• *Frontal shot, side view, three-quarters frontal, back or rear view.*

Then there is an indication of the camera's height (actual or apparent) –
• *Low shot, level shot, high shot,* and even *top or overhead shot.*

Sometimes a general direction such as –
• *'Over-shoulder shot'* or *'point-of-view shot' (POV)* is sufficient indication.

For some purposes it is enough simply to indicate how many people are to be in the shot, and use the general guides –
• *'Single shot', 'two shot', 'three shot'* or even a *'group shot'.*
The shot will be framed to just accommodate that number.

Terminology
Although the basic shots are universal, unfortunately the terminology used to define them can vary from one place to the next. So for example, while one director talks about a *'bust shot'* or a *'chest shot'* another wants an *'MCU'.* To avoid confusion it is best to stick to those used locally.

The easiest way to remember these standard shots is by the way they are framed: e.g. 'cutting just below the waist', 'just below the knees'. . . In no time at all, you will find yourself automatically thinking in these terms, free to concentrate on other aspects of the camerawork.

68

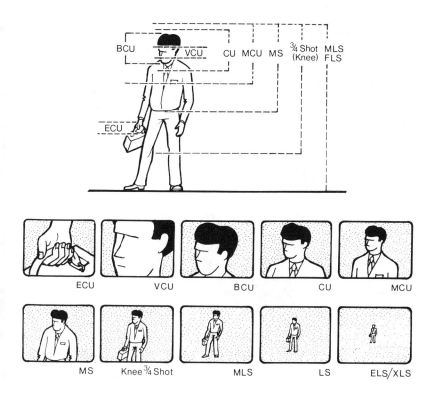

Shots are identified by how much of the subject they include:

ECU Extreme close-up (detail shot) – isolated detail.
VCU Very close-up (face shot) – from mid-forehead to above chin.
BCU Big close-up (tight CU, full head) – full head height nearly fills the screen.
CU Close-up – just above head to upper chest (cuts below necktie knot).
MCU Medium close-up (bust shot, chest shot) – cuts body at lower chest (breast pocket, armpit).
MS Medium shot (mid-shot, close medium shot, CMS, waist shot) – cuts body just below waist.
Knee, ¾ shot Knee shot, three-quarter length shot – cuts just below knees.
MLS Medium long shot (full-length shot, FLS) – entire body plus short distance above/below.
LS Long shot – person occupies three-quarters to one-third screen height.
ELS Extra long shot (extreme LS, XLS).

Unkind Shots

There are a few people whom the camera loves! Somehow, no matter how harsh the lighting, however sparse the make-up or critical the camera's scrutiny, these people always look great! But for most of us, the camera has the ability to misshapen and distort our features, until even our nearest and dearest are lost for words.

Let's see how the camera manages to emphasize physical shortcomings and distort one's appearance.

Lens angle
Since a narrow-angle lens appears to compress depth, and a wide-angle lens to exaggerate depth, it is not surprising that your choice of lens angles can have a considerable influence on the way three-dimensional features are reproduced. Try for yourself, the effects of using an inappropriate lens angle on a willing subject.

• *Wide-angle* – If you get too close with a wide-angle lens, a person's nose and chin will become prominent in a full-face shot; the head's roundness will be emphasized and their forehead will recede. The result is so grotesque, that you are unlikely to use this technique for serious portraiture! However, when you are shooting in very restricted surroundings (e.g. an elevator) you may well be tempted to use a close wide-angle lens, just in order to get the shot... so be warned!

• *Narrow-angle lens* – It is sometimes argued that for certain types of face (e.g. people with deep-set eyes) narrower lens angles produce more attractively proportioned features. But the facial compression and loss of modeling that very narrow lens angles produce in close-ups of distant people, is hardly flattering. In full-face shots, the nose tends to squash, while the forehead and chin look more prominent. The overall flattening effect resembles that of a photo cut-out. Notwithstanding these limitations, when you need close shots on a distant camera, distortions of this kind just have to be accepted.

Camera height
The height of the camera's viewpoint can affect a person's appearance in several ways. Shots that look down on someone, tend to emphasize baldness, plumpness, large bosoms, and cause them to look shorter and less imposing.

From a low viewpoint, people look more impressive, more powerful. But in closer shots, the camera tends to emphasize noses, particularly where the person has large, uptilted or dilated nostrils. Lower shots also draw attention to scrawny necks and heavy jawlines, and rotundity. A high forehead or receding hair, may appear completely bald in a low shot.

Background influence
An inappropriate background can draw attention to the subject's less attractive features.

Shooting from above
High-angle (elevated) shots can be unflattering by emphasizing foreheads and baldness, and reducing effective height, which often makes people look weak and lacking in authority.

Shooting from below
Low-angle (depressed) shots can draw attention to other less attractive features – scrawny neck, deep-set eyes, nostrils, and can suggest baldness with a high hairline.

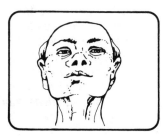

Long Shots

You will generally want to use *long shots* —
- To *follow* wide-ranging or fast action.
- When subjects are *spread* over a wide area.
- To show *where* the action is taking place.
- When you want to emphasize *extent*, i.e. to reveal how large, how crowded, or how extensive an area is (e.g. in a busy airport)
- To show *progress*; i.e. how far the climber has reached.
- To display an *atmospheric effect*, e.g. show a magnificent interior.
- To establish the *time* or *season*; e.g. falling snow beyond a window.
- To show how one subject's *position* is related to another's.

Shot preferences
On the small TV screen, long shots give us an overall impression. Obviously they cannot show detail. A well balanced program sequence needs distant and closer views of the action. Which type of shot predominates, will depend on the kind of production you are working on. In a horse race for example, emphasis is on long shots; while for a demonstration of flower arrangement, close shots are essential.

Camera operation
In long shots there is usually considerable depth of field, so focusing is easy. However, you are unlikely to be able to pan or tilt the camera much – especially in the studio – without finding that you are shooting beyond the main acting area, and seeing extraneous subjects (e.g. bystanders, lamps, other cameras), or overshooting the edges of the setting.

If you are using a *wide-angle* lens to get the long shot, it is likely that perspective will be exaggerated, and there may be obvious geometrical distortions near picture edges.

Dollying and *trucking* are not particularly effective in long shots, but big changes in camera height can still be dramatic.

Lens flare
When you are shooting into lights, or where lamps are just outside the shot pointing towards the camera, *lens flares* and inter-lens reflections are a regular hazard. They are all too obvious on a color monitor, but may be barely discernible in a camera's black-and-white viewfinder. These visual blemishes take the form of spurious rays, blobs or patches of light, or an overall greying (*setting up*) affecting the entire picture. Although a camera's *flare corrector* circuits can improve the last, the only sure remedy is to avoid shooting into lights wherever possible, and to fit an efficient *lens shade* (*lens hood*).

Space

Where confined space prevents you getting a long enough shot, camera distance can often be increased by shooting in through a door or window.

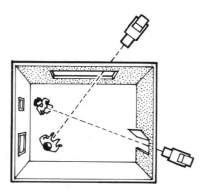

Overshoot

Cameras can easily overshoot past the edges of the action area and include unwanted items in the shot.

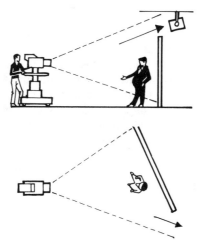

Medium Shots

Quite a wide range of shots can be called 'medium'. Typically they cover people from 'three-quarter length (knee) shots' to 'mid' shots. The productional value of a medium shot lies somewhere between that of longer shots in which the surroundings predominate, and closer shots in which the viewer concentrates on the subject and ignores whatever else is nearby. Medium shots allow the audience to see both the performer/talent and their surroundings clearly.

Camera operation
In a medium shot, you can still keep quite large gestures, arm and body movements within the frame. When the subject moves around a little, there is usually no need to re-focus or to re-frame the shot

Depth of field is sufficient at typical working lens apertures (e.g. around f/5·6) for you to keep the subject sharply focused, while leaving the background details slightly softened. As you tighten the shot, the surroundings become less distinct and lose their impact – so the subject itself becomes more prominent, and isolated from its surroundings.

With medium shots you can move the camera around smoothly on shot (using a normal to wide lens angle). You can adjust camera height unobtrusively, particularly if camera movements are *motivated* by action in the scene; e.g. someone getting up and going over to open a door.

Audience interest
For the director, the *medium shot* provides a safe, uncritical, general-purpose viewpoint. It offers the audience a useful amount of detailed information and so can sustain interest for a relatively long time.

While *long shots* give your audience the opportunity to glance around a scene freely, eventually they will want to take a closer look at whatever catches their attention.

A *close shot* restricts how much the viewer can see, and so concentrates the attention. But it normally only holds interest for a comparatively short period.

Medium shots

Theses have various important features. They enable the viewer to see a reasonable amount of detail in the subject, while at the same time revealing its surroundings. So the environment, lighting etc. make a strong impact. Medium shots can contain a considerable amount of action without requiring adjustment of the camera's position.

Close Shots

As you take closer and closer shots of a subject, camerawork becomes increasingly critical. The technique you use to get these shots will affect the sort of problems you are likely to have.

Regular problems
• We saw earlier, how a close *wide-angle lens* can appear to distort a subject as it exaggerates its depth and modeling. There is also the danger that the close camera's shadow will fall onto the subject.

• Use a *narrow-angle lens* further away, and these problems will disappear. Instead, you may find that you are now limited by the lens's *minimum focused distance* (*MFD*). Here you find that you have come to the end of the focus control's adjustment, yet still cannot sharply focus the image. The only solution is to move the subject or camera further away, or use a wider lens angle (shorter focal length).

Coarse camera handling with the narrow-angle lens can make it hard to control the exact framing of close-up shots of distant subjects.

Typical spatial flattening can considerably distort a distant subject's appearance.

Depth of field
Depth is so restricted in close shots, that you will often have to decide whether to *accept* the situation, *split focus*, or try to *increase depth* by –

• *Stopping down*, which will mean that much more light will be needed.

• *Taking a wider shot*, and accepting the smaller subject image.

Subject movement
Although you may sometimes allow parts of a subject to move out of shot, you should normally try to contain all subject movement within the frame.

The closer the shot, the more difficult it becomes to cope with movement. Focusing and framing become erratic, and because the subject fills a large area of the screen, any inaccuracies become very obvious.

Confining the subject
For very close shots, the subject needs to be held perfectly steady to allow details to be seen clearly. Wherever possible, use a marked table-top position on which the item can be laid or supported firmly.

For extremely close shots (e.g. of a postage stamp), turn the zoom lens to the *macro* position – although you will no longer be able to zoom. Otherwise fit a clip-on *supplementary lens* (*diopter lens*) which will narrow (*negative*) or widen (*positive*) the effective lens angle.

Shot limits

In very close shots, action should be kept within the frame area, avoiding movements in/out of shot.

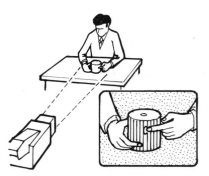

Shallow depth

Although depth of field is limited in close shots, you can make the most of it by ensuring that important surfaces are at right angles to the lens axis. If a flat surface is tilted, parts of it can fall outside the focused zone and become defocused.

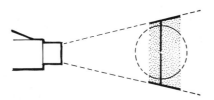

Calculating shots

A lot of directors and camera operators prefer to work empirically. Knowing the focal length of the lens and the camera distance, they can make a shrewd guess whether they will be able to get the sort of shot they want from a particular viewpoint. A director who wants to check out potential shots during pre-studio rehearsals, will often look at the action through a small adjustable viewfinder, which shows the shot-sizes that different lens angles will give.

Measuring the shot

That's fine when you have something to look at. But what do you do when planning and estimating production treatment before the studio settings have been built? The answer is to use a scale plan of the setting, the studio or the location, and simply lay a transparent protractor at the probable camera position. Then you can see the exact coverage of any lens angle. But what if there is no scale plan?

Then all you have to do, is to check the range of lens angles your zoom lens covers, and look up the graph opposite. There you will see at a glance the shots you will get at various distances. This avoids laborious calculations, pages of tables, or trial and error. You can extend the scales by multiplying them by two or more.

If for example, you know that someone is 3 m/ 10 ft away, it shows immediately that if you want a close-up, you will need a lens angle of just over 10°. If your narrowest angle happens to be 20°, you will have to move closer, to around 2·5 m/ 8 ft from the subject to get the shot.

How to use the graph

• *To see the shot you will get* – Draw a vertical line up from the *camera distance* to the *lens angle* being used. The shot you get is shown on the *left* scale.

• *To see how far away you need to be* – Choose the *shot size* you want on the vertical scale. Then follow a horizontal line across to the *lens angle* you are going to use, then down to the *distance scale* below.

• *To find the lens angle needed* – Draw a line up from the *distance scale*, then another across from the *shot size* you want. Where they meet, you have the *lens angle* needed.

• *To find the width of the scene in shot* – Look up from the *distance* to the *lens angle* being used. Where it meets this angle, look across to the *vertical scale* on the left, where you will see the shot *width*. (The *shot height* is three-quarters of the width.)

• *Filling certain proportions of the screen* – If for example, you want an object to take up one-third of the frame width, simply multiply *the width of your subject* by three in this case, and find the *camera distance* and *lens angle* needed for that width.

78

Lens angle

Horizontal	Vertical
5°	3.75°
10°	7.5°
15°	11.25°
20°	15°
25°	18.75°
30°	22.5°
35°	26.25°
40°	30°
45°	34°
50°	37.5°
55°	40.25°
60°	45°

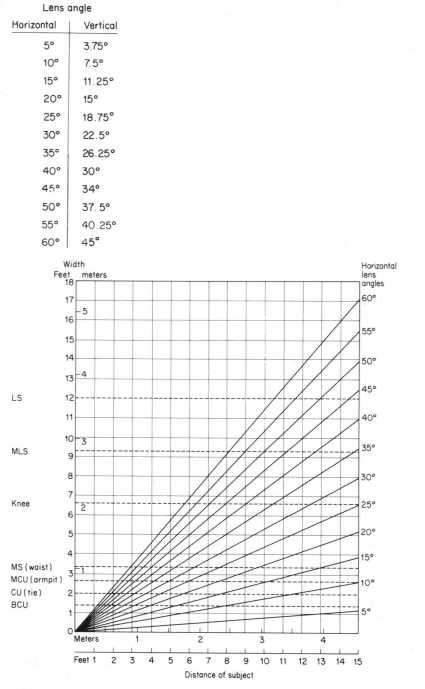

Universal camera set-up graph
The graph shows, at a glance, details of obtainable shots. For greater or shorter
distance, just multiply or divide the scale readings.

The Picture Frame

We are so willing to accept the flat framed image on our TV screens as 'real', that we tend to overlook how artificial it actually is. We have become accustomed to the various strange effects we see there, and now regard them as 'natural'!

The two-dimensional world
The *flat screen* and the restrictive *frame* around the picture, can produce some very strange illusions, which directly influence our interpretation of what we are looking at:

- Subjects that are some distance apart, can appear joined together – e.g. a distant post appearing to 'grow' out of someone's head.
- The apparent shapes and sizes of objects in the scene can vary with the lens angle and the subject's distance (*perspective distortion*).
- The effects of tone and color can change dramatically. Even a small area of brilliant color can dominate a shot if it is near the camera . . . yet become insignificant if the lens angle or the viewpoint changes.
- A surface's apparent tone and color can depend on its effective size, clarity, texture, the angle and color of the light, and the surroundings.
- A number of subjects can seem to be grouped together in a unified group or forming a pattern, simply as a result of the camera's viewpoint.
- The frame can appear to interact with subjects near the picture's edge; restricting, crushing down, cutting them off, drawing them outwards.
- A picture's balance will vary as you reposition a subject in the frame.

Tight and loose framing
In *tight close-ups*, the frame seems to confine and obstruct the subject. *Very loose framing* leaves considerable space around the subject, and can give an impression of isolation, emptiness, space.

Headroom
If there is *too little* room between the top of a person's head and the top of the frame, a shot looks cramped. *Too much*, and it looks bottom-heavy. Even a slight tilt of the camera alters the headroom considerably. The closer the shot, the less the headroom needed. But it should be consistent between similar shot sizes, and between different cameras' pictures.

Receiver masking
Although viewfinders show the entire picture, TV receivers are often *overscanned* so that picture edges are lost beyond the screen surround. Avoid placing items or titling near the frame edges, or they may be cut off.

Headroom

The space between heads and the top of frame should be adjusted for attractive vertical balance, (a). It should not be excessive as in (c) which gives a bottom-heavy effect, not too little as in (b) which gives a cramped effect.

Safety margins

Any subjects falling near picture borders are liable to be masked off by the TV receiver. So keep action and titles within the safe areas.

Tight frames

On very close shots, subjects can easily move outside the frame.

Framing the Shot

When you are setting up any shot, always ask yourself:
- *What is just outside the frame? It may be important – or about to intrude.*
- *How do the subjects interact with the frame in this shot?*

Avoid routine centering

Although at first sight the most logical thing to do, is to place your main subject in the *center* of the screen, that is not always the most effective way of presenting it. In practice, the center of the screen has been found to be the *weakest* concentrational area. The eye tends to move away from it towards other parts of the shot, unless there are;
- strong compositional lines concentrating on it,
- or eye-catching movement, color or form.

Most subjects look best when *off-centered* to some extent, balanced against other tonal masses in the picture.

Offset framing

A *centrally-framed* subject can look too deliberately balanced, formal, even dull. If someone is speaking directly to the camera, the picture will often look much more attractive if their body is slightly angled – e.g. facing a three-quarter frontal position, with the framing *offset* a little to compensate. The amount of this offset or '*looking-room*' should generally be increased with the subject's angle, as they turn towards a profile.

The rule of thirds

Except for special effects, it is best to avoid splitting the screen into equal, evenly balanced sections. The result is far too mechanical. To avoid this, many camera operators regularly use a routine called *the rule of thirds*. Here you divide the screen into thirds vertically and horizontally, and put subjects on these lines, or wherever they cross. Although better than using a bisected frame, this too can become a very predictable device.

In general, you will get much more satisfying proportions if you use either 2:3 (fifths) or 3:5 (eighths) ratios, for these approximate more closely to the *Golden Section* so widely applied in the graphic arts.

Framing people

If you are not careful, people can look as if they are sitting, leaning or standing on the border of the picture. So look out for this situation. It can be distracting – even ridiculous. Check too, that the frame does not cut the body and limbs at *natural joins* (neck, knees, elbows), for this too draws attention to itself. Instead, arrange for the frame to cut at the intermediate points you see in the diagram opposite.

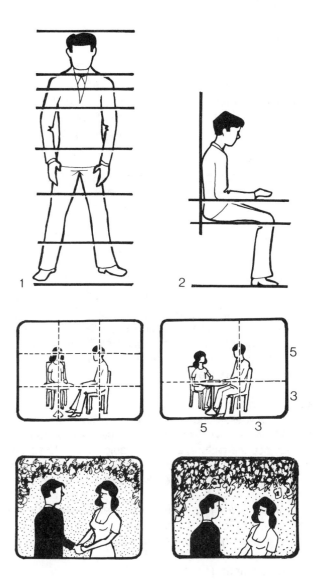

Framing faults
Avoid (1) letting the frame cut people at natural joints. Choose intermediate places, as shown here. Avoid them touching the screen edges (2).

Proportions
Dividing the screen into thirds produces standard, uninteresting proportions. Ratios of 3:5 or 2:3 give a more pleasing balance.

Ambiguous framing
If too prominent, a nearby subject may appear important. Is there someone hiding in the tree?

83

Reframing

As people move around, or the point of interest in the picture changes, you normally need to reframe the shot to compensate. This might involve little more than a slight tilt to correct the headroom, or a simultaneous *pan–tilt–zoom* to tighten on a single person within a group shot.

Reframe during movement
The most successful camerawork always looks as if it has developed quite naturally from the action itself. If you alter the shot by reframing, tilting, panning, zooming or dollying on a *motionless subject* your audience will be aware of the change immediately. But make these adjustments while the subject itself is *moving* (even a head turn will do), and the camerawork will still be effective – but quite unobtrusive.

People enter the frame
If a person in a close shot is joined by someone else, there is obviously not room for them both without crowding the frame. So directors will often cut at that point to a wider two-shot shot. But what if there isn't a second camera, or this cut would interrupt the visual flow? The solution is to zoom out (or dolly back) as the newcomer enters the frame, while panning over slightly to offset the first person.

People leave the frame
When someone walks out of a shot, you have three options:
- *To center up on whoever remains* – Panning away from the person exiting, to rebalance the picture; a smooth, quick and unhesitating action.
- *To move in before they exit* – At the end of a sequence, the camera can move in to a speaker; excluding the second person who leaves when no longer seen.
- *To hold the frame still* – Here you just let them move out of frame, and continue to hold the shot. This deliberately leaves the shot temporarily unbalanced, emphasizing their departure.

Maintaining good framing
Trying to hold a very tight shot on a fast or randomly moving subject, is a recipe for disaster! Sometimes it can't be avoided of course . . . and might just come off! However, even when the action is fairly predictable – such as someone on a swing or a rocking-chair, the result is usually not all that rewarding. Frame-chasing tight shots are tiring to watch, particularly if the subject keeps passing out of the frame. It is better to widen the shot, so that movements can be followed more accurately.

Adjustment
As people enter or leave the frame, you should normally readjust the framing.

Held frame
Sometimes a dramatic point is made by deliberately holding the frame still after an exit, to emphasize someone's departure.

The Basics of Composition

Composition is the technique of arranging pictures so that they not only please the eye, but create a deliberate emotional impact, directing the audience's attention to particular parts of the scene.

Line
Whether the various lines running through a picture are *real* (structural or painted), or *imaginary* (formed by arrangements of objects or people), they will influence the viewers' feelings about what they are seeing. Compositional lines (e.g. perspective) lead the eye within the picture.
- *Vertical straight lines* give an impression of formality, height, restriction.
- *Horizontals* can impart a feeling of breadth, openness, stability, rest.

If you take a straight-on shot of a scene containing such lines, the picture will reflect these characteristics.

Supposing you move to a more oblique viewpoint. Now the same lines can appear in the picture as *diagonals*; lines which are inherently more arresting, interesting. The same subjects now look dynamic, exciting, forceful, even unstable.
- *Curved lines* convey an impression of beauty, elegance, movement, visual rhythm – although they can also look weak.

Tone
Whether tonal areas in the scene are *direct* (a wall covering, clothing), or *indirect* (through light and shade due to light distribution) they directly affect the mood and pictorial balance of a shot.
- *Light-toned backgrounds* –The effect is simple, cheerful, delicate, lively, open.
- *Dark-toned backgrounds* – Generally dramatic, somber, forceful, even drab.

Under different lighting the apparent tone of a mid-gray surface can be made to range from white to black.

Background tones (and colors) can affect the apparent tones of the subject itself; seeming lighter against dark, darker against light.

Balance
An attractively composed picture is usually *balanced* about its center. Balance is affected by tonal values, their size, shape and relative positions in the frame. It may be *symmetrical* (looking formal, simple, but comparatively monotonous), or *asymmetrical* (where lighter-weight areas near the frame edge, counterbalance heavier ones nearer the center).

Unity
This is the principle of arranging subjects within the frame as interrelated groups, rather than scattered around as separate items.

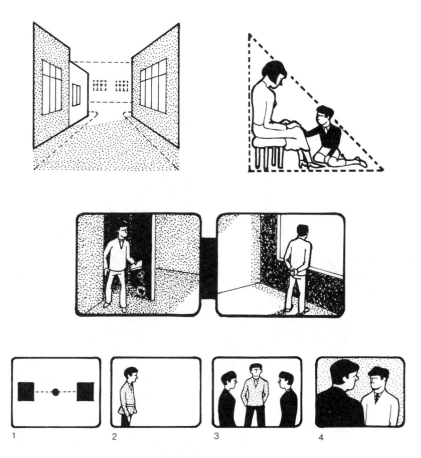

Line
Lines creating shapes and patterns direct the eye in the picture. These lines may be *real*, forming an actual part of the scene. Here converging lines draw attention to the distant building. Lines may also be entirely *imaginary* but felt to be there as we look at a picture, as with this 'triangle', which seems to give the subject stability and unity.

Tone
Tones influence how we respond to a picture. Darker tones give an enclosed feeling compared with the open effect of light tones in the second picture. Against darker tones, light-toned clothing is more prominent.

Balance
1. Shots need to be balanced around the picture centre.
2. Lack of balance makes the picture appear attractively unstable.
3. A formally balanced picture with a symmetrical arrangement can look uninteresting and monotonous.
4. By adjusting the size and position of tonal areas in the picture (by careful positioning and framing) a more attractive effect is achieved.

87

Practical Composition

Although the artist with a blank canvas has a free choice in arranging shapes, texture, color, etc., you are working in the real world, and have to compose pictures from whatever is there in the scene.

Sometimes you may be able to rearrange the subject, repositioning or adjusting to improve the shot. But more often, you have to rely on selecting just the right viewpoint, adjusting perspective, and careful framing to compose your picture effectively. If you do this skillfully, the result will be so convincing that it all seems to have happened naturally. If a shot is badly composed it will look muddled, allowing the viewer's attention to wander, failing to hold their interest. Where shots are too obviously 'organized', they are likely to look contrived, stylized, or mechanical.

Adjusting composition

Some directors work out the composition of master shots beforehand with *storyboard sketches*, others rely on you to provide appropriately composed pictures from pre-arranged camera positions. It varies with individuals and the type of production you are working on. In most cases you will find that you have to compose shots on-the-hoof using whatever opportunities you find. At first sight this may seem to offer little scope, but in practice, you can alter visual emphasis in several ways:

• *By adjusting subject size* – Depending on the length of shot you choose, a subject may dominate, or recede into the background. Certain foreground features can appear prominent, strong, or quite incidental.

• *By adjusting framing* – Framing will determine exactly how much of the action is visible to your audience. You can include/exclude parts of the subject, and select how much they see of the surroundings and other things nearby. If something is kept out of the shot, the viewer may not even realize that it exists! Careful framing can create tension by restricting information.

Even slight reframing can alter the entire compositional balance of a shot:

• *By adjusting proportions* – By making subtle changes in the lens angle and the camera distance, you can alter the relative proportions of a subject and its background.

• *By choosing the lens height carefully* – The camera's height can strengthen or weaken a subject's impact. You can use foreground items to frame the shot; or deliberately exclude them if they are intrusive.

• *By moving sideways a little* – By moving the camera to one side, you may be able to prevent a foreground subject from obscuring (*masking*) another that is further away. Similarly, a slight lateral move may help you to avoid something that is intruding into the shot.

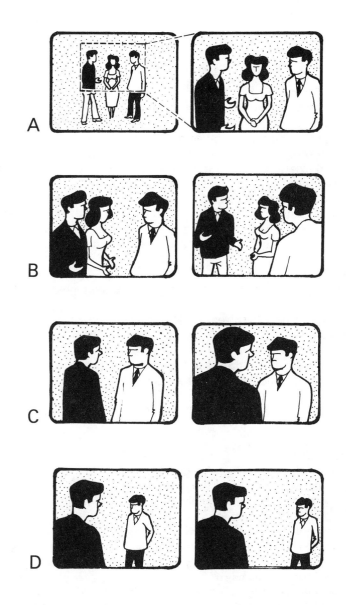

Adjusting composition
A. By adjusting shot size, the relative visual impacts of the subject and its surroundings are altered.
B. By slightly changing the camera position (trucking), the picture balance can be altered.
C. By adjusting the lens angle and camera distance, proportions can be changed.
D. By moving to new viewpoint, the subject grouping (visual unity) can appear quite different.

Composing in Depth

Although the TV screen can only show us a *flat* image of the three-dimensional world, the audience gets a very convincing impression of depth and distance, thanks to the various visual clues they can see. They subconsciously interpret space by comparing relative sizes, converging lines (*linear perspective*), seeing how one plane overlaps another (*masking*) and how the relative positions of subjects change as the camera moves (*parallactic movement*).

A picture with a strong impression of depth, holds the interest, and is usually more convincing and attractive, than one which is flat and even-toned. If there are few visual clues to depth in a picture, it can be hard to judge scale, space and distances (e.g. as in open desert landscapes).

Enhancing depth
There are several ways in which you can give a picture a greater feeling of depth and realism:
• Try to avoid having the subject isolated against a plain background, particularly where the lighting is flat and diffused, or shining from behind the camera (*dead frontal*).
• Where there are familiar-sized subjects in the shot (people, furniture) the viewer will get a better idea of distance and scale.
• When the camera shoots through clearly-defined foreground planes, such as foliage or a window-frame, the illusion of depth is considerably enhanced.

Aim at natural effects
Whenever you select or arrange foreground subjects to improve scenic depth, introduce them as naturally as possible. Effective enough when they *are* appropriate (e.g. the viewpoint of a person in hiding), they can become too obtrusive if overdone.

Resist the temptation to use foreground pieces habitually, in shot after shot – 'just to complete the picture'. And steer clear of a 'peek-a-boo' camera style, in which you continually shoot the subject through grass, bead curtains, holes in a fence . . .

Another favorite trick that can be overused, is to begin a shot with a clearly focused image of an unimportant foreground object (such as a wayside flower), then pull focus dramatically to blur it completely, bringing the real subject which is in the distance into sharp focus (e.g. a car speeding along on the highway).

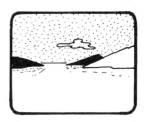

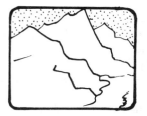

The illusion of depth
Foregrounds can help to create a greater impression of depth, distance and scale, particularly for isolated, remote subjects.

Foreground planes
Where the camera shoots the action beyond a foreground plane such as a window, screen, foliage, this can form a natural border to the picture.

Concentrating Attention

The more there is to see in a picture, the greater the opportunity for the audience's attention to wander. Although the director occasionally invites the audience to simply browse around, looking at whatever catches their interest, more often the aim is to persuade them to concentrate on certain features in the scene, to watch what someone is doing, to listen to what they are saying; and not be diverted by whatever is going on in the background.

There are certainly times when you should not let the audience see too much! If during a street interview for instance, they can read posters, see children waving to camera, watch the passing traffic . . . they are unlikely to be paying full attention to what is being said.

Focusing interest
There are various ways of persuading an audience to look at a particular subject – a remark, a gesture, emphasized lighting. But the camera too can do a great deal to center their interest:
- Take *close shots*, which exclude nearby distractions.
- Select a *plain background* for the subject, or limit the depth of field to isolate it (*differential focusing*).
- Avoid *weak shots* – side or rear views, high or distant shots.
- Introduce *movement* – dollying, zooming, arcing around the subject.
- Arrange *composition* so that it draws attention to the subject – isolating it, giving it prominence, adjusting balance, converging lines, etc.
- Frame the shot carefully, to keep unwanted subjects out of shot.

Overdoing it
If you try to concentrate attention by filling the screen with enlarged detail, you may find that the picture loses impact because it –
- Reveals *coarseness* (the half-tone dots of old newspaper photographs; the line formation of engravings).
- Loses *clarity* (over-enlarging an unsharp photograph).
- Gives a minor feature *over-prominence*, relative to the main subject.

Peeking through
Where you are having to shoot through wire mesh, foliage, etc., for a view of a subject, these obstructions may become a defocused blur, or even disappear altogether, if you keep the lens close to them. It is better though, wherever possible, to keep them out of shot altogether, for even an indistinguishable blur will degrade the overall image to some extent.

Foreground obstructions
Rather than including distracting foreground foliage, netting etc. in a shot, get closer and shoot through it. Even if you cannot avoid it altogether, this method makes it indistinct and less obtrusive.

Prominent subjects
Where a foreground subject is too prominent, better proportions are often achieved by shooting further away with a narrower lens angle.

Hiding distracting objects
By choosing the camera position carefully you can often hide distracting background objects behind people.

Inappropriate Shots

You can see inappropriate shots of one kind or another every day on your home TV. Even professionals aren't infallible! Shots can be inappropriate in several ways:

- *Unclear subject* – The camera may not be showing the subject clearly; the shot is too distant, too close, at the wrong angle. (For example, a cook is pointing out *detail* – but the director takes a *long shot* !)
- *Unseen subject* – The shot does not show us what a person is speaking about. (A speaker refers to details in a book illustration – which is not shown by the camera.)
- *Poor composition* – The shot directs attention to the wrong subject.
- *Inept* – The shot may be overdramatic, or miss visual opportunities.

Stylized camerawork
In the same way that you can provide characterless illumination by just flooding a scene with light, you can use the camera as a hack tool that provides routine shots from routine viewpoints – zooming in and out to avoid the labor (and skill) of appropriate camera movements.

On the other hand it is a fact of life, that certain production assignments do follow a standard pattern, and if you are tempted to 'improve' a perfectly normal interview by getting unusual dramatic shots, they are unlikely to be welcomed by the director

What may seem a 'great shot' can draw disproportionate attention to itself. It may over-emphasize. It may be out of place. Dramatic shots and fast intercutting in a cookery demonstration, might have the audience holding their breath, waiting for the frying pan to catch fire, rather than watching culinary techniques!

A low-angle shot may show a speaker as imposing or threatening. But what if she is only giving a weather forecast? A canted shot has the power to convey instability or madness. But introduce it into a demonstration of farm machinery, and the shot impact is quite inappropriate. It means nothing, and will merely puzzle the audience.

Dubious treatment
Another bogus type of camerawork, is the 'significantly composed' shot, where a prominent foreground object has been used to provide 'strong composition', but succeeds only in dominating the picture.

A good camera operator interprets the director's ideas, rather than pushing his/her own. If a director is inexperienced, most will judge when to follow instructions exactly, and when to suggest alternative approaches. (*'Wouldn't it be better if . . .'*) Where directors insist on unwise techniques, that is their responsibility.

Overdramatizing

Dramatic shots are fine, provided they are used at appropriate times.

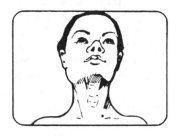

Contrived shots

'Significantly composed' shots too easily look bogus and simply draw attention to their own cleverness.

Problem Shots

Even quite simple situations can pose some surprisingly tricky problems.

The wrong shape
How do you shoot subjects that are tall, round, long ... with a camera that has a constant horizontal four-by-three picture shape?

If you do the obvious, and take an overall view of the subject, this will show its general form, but important details will probably not be clear. If you concentrate on the details, there is always the chance that your audience will not realize how these relate to the whole.

One major difficulty is that you often cannot get far enough away from a large subject, before other things nearby get in the way and spoil the shot. In some situations, even quite a small object in the foreground can obscure a large subject in the distance.

Although you may find that a wide-angle shot will cover the entire subject from a reasonable distance, it will probably distort its shape and proportions and give a very false idea of distances. This is very obvious when shooting upwards at skyscrapers. Paradoxically, the foreshortening and strong perspective can produce a very powerful arresting image; but if the picture's purpose is to show structural information and proportions, it is likely to be less than successful.

One solution when shooting a large subject is to begin with an overall view. This long shot gives the audience an idea of its general form. Then take a series of closer shots showing its main features in some detail.

As an alternative, you might select a viewpoint looking along the subject, then pan over it slowly, or shoot it progressively in sections.

Spread subjects
Where things are spread around, you may have some difficulty bringing them together in the same shot. Let's consider a couple of people sitting at either end of a long table. Avoid panning to and fro between the subjects. This '*hosepiping*' over empty space looks very crude. An oblique end-on shot (perhaps an *over-shoulder* view) is better, for it helps the audience to maintain their sense of direction. Otherwise the answer is to take a long shot, then rely on intercut individual close-ups.

Shooting into lights
Apart from deliberate effects (glare, flares, silhouettes) it is best to avoid shooting into lights. (It can ruin camera tubes!) Light shining straight into the lens tends to degrade the image, and affect exposure. To prevent lens flares, try extending the *lens hood* (*sun shade*), or raise the camera and tilt down.

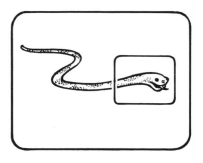

The wrong shape

Many subjects do not fit the screen's four by three format at all well. They are too tall, wide, long, or the wrong shape. Such subjects have to be shot in a wide view and then in localised segments.

Spread subjects

When subjects are spaced wide apart, you can often group them together in a well-balanced shot by using carefully selected viewpoints.

Changing Camera Height

There will be odd occasions when you need extreme heights such as worm's-eye or bird's-eye views, steep upward-angled shots, high viewpoints, but most situations require only modest height variations.

Pedestals

On some pedestals, the central column's height is pre-adjusted with a hand-crank while off shot. More versatile are the lightweight pedestals with pneumatically balanced columns which are easily readjusted, even while shooting.

Remember, the pedestal's column needs to be vertically balanced to suit the overall weight of the camera, viewfinder, prompter, and other accessories. Correct balance ensures height adjustments are smooth and easy. This may involve changing counter-balance weights or altering the gas pressure. Once balanced, you can raise and lower the camera imperceptibly slowly with precision, or dramatically fast – taking care of course, not to hit the column limits and jar the camera!

Why alter camera height?

The camera height you select usually depends on whether you want a natural or dramatic effect. For high or low positions, you will need to tilt the viewfinder so that you can see its screen comfortably.

When shooting people, the best camera height is normally around their *eye-level*.

- For a person who is *standing* that may be about 1·2 – 1·5 m (4 – 5 ft).
- For someone who is *sitting* it is typically 1·1 m (3·5 ft).

Although you might shoot down or up at an actor in a dramatic situation, for everyday occasions the effects would be inappropriate.

Where the performer/talent is up on a platform (*parallel, rostrum*), the base of the camera mounting may not be able to get nearer that 1 m/3 ft to its edge. Unlike *jib arms* or *camera cranes*, a pedestal has little or no front overhang, and that will limit the closeness and range of shots possible.

Unexpected effects

If you raise the camera and tilt down at the same time, while holding the subject center-frame, the distant floor will look as if it is *tilting forward*! Doing the reverse and lowering the camera while tilting upwards, produces a *tilt-away* effect. The greater the height change, the more pronounced this illusion.

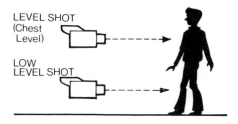

LEVEL SHOT
(Chest
Level)

LOW
LEVEL SHOT

Level shots

The 'normal' camera viewpoint is usually around chest height. For somebody standing, this is about 1.2–1.8m (4–5ft) from the floor. For a seated person, the camera is typically 1.1m (3.5ft) high.

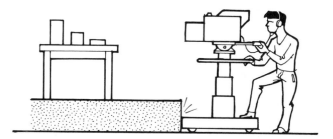

Obstructions

Platforms (rostra), steps and uneven ground impede most camera dollies. Although the jib of a crane can stretch over such obstructions, a pedestal or rolling tripod may, for example, be unable to approach and look down on a table.

High Shots

A *high-angle* shot has the very practical advantage that it allows the camera to see over things that would otherwise obstruct the picture. However, high viewpoints can present unflattering weak shots of people. You can never get a strong, powerful shot of a person from a high camera position.

Working with a high camera
When shooting within a crowd, holding a lightweight camera above your head with arms outstretched may get by in an emergency, but it is not a recommended technique. The strain is considerable, and shots will inevitably be shaky. It is far better to climb up to a higher vantage point, and hold the camera properly.

A high tripod or pedestal will support a camera firmly up to a height of around 1·5 – 2 m (5 – 6 ft). But the controls of most cameras are not easy to operate at maximum elevation. In addition, you may be unable to see into the viewfinder screen properly. It will often help if you stand on a pedestal's base, or on a box (*riser, block*).

It is unrealistic to expect a single operator to move the pedestal around at maximum height while on shot with any sort of accuracy. If the camera needs to *dolly* (*track*), *truck* (*crab*) or *arc*, then a second person is needed to push and guide it. But it's an unreliable process.

Even if your *viewfinder* is well shielded from stray light and tilted down, you may still find yourself looking up towards a bright sky or into studio lights. That will make it much more difficult to follow focusing accurately.

There is a world of difference between operating an *extendable jib arm* mounted on a tripod or pedestal, and a *camera crane*. Remotely controlling the jib camera while watching a monitor is a 'detached' process, compared with the more integrated feeling when sitting on a crane. Although the jib camera can swing round an arc of 360°, and change height from e.g. 0·3 – 3 m (1 – 10 ft), a director would be unwise to expect the camera to focus, pan, tilt, zoom, boom up and move around at the same time! When working at full height, there is always the hazard of the camera colliding with overhanging lights, scenery, cables.

Problems with high shots
As the camera rises, it sees more and more of the floor. Because we are accustomed to seeing a foreshortened view of space (like a camera at eye level), the floor area looks disproportionally large and less impressive on high shots; particularly when using a wide lens angle. A high close camera is very likely to shadow a subject.

Terms

High-angle shots tend to reduce the strength of a subject but give a clearer view of the action. They may be shot from an elevated camera or via a slung mirror or from a raised vantage point – e.g. a platform or tower.

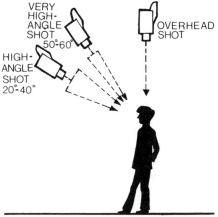

VERY HIGH-ANGLE SHOT 50°-60°

HIGH-ANGLE SHOT 20°-40°

OVERHEAD SHOT

The effects of height changes

As the camera moves to a higher viewpoint, the floor becomes more prominent and the audience often feels less involved in the action.

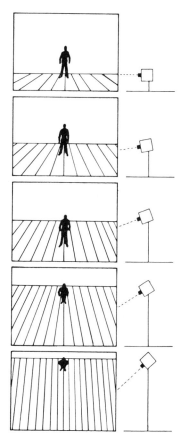

Low Shots

Whenever you shoot down onto a subject the viewpoint may appear natural enough, but it will not necessarily show the subject itself most effectively. It may be better to raise the subject up until it is nearer to the normal camera height, (e.g. place it on a table), or lower the camera so that its viewpoint is level with the subject.

When you are shooting something on the ground, you will get much more striking pictures if the camera is around floor level (a *ground shot*), than with a down-tilted camera at the normal height. But will this 'dog's-eye' view appear strange or inappropriate in the context of the program?

The effect of low viewpoints

Most subjects tend to look impressive or important if you shoot them from *just below* the normal eye-line. But take care, for some can take on a very strange and uncharacteristic appearance and turn into 'puzzle pictures'! When you shoot upwards from a *very low angle*, you will often find that the background dominates or even overwhelms many subjects.

Shot from a low angle, a person can be made to appear imposing, threatening, powerful. Even their most innocent actions – a glance, an outstretched arm – can seem significant. If you are using a wide-angle lens, this effect will be exaggerated even further. So from an artistic point of view, always select low camera positions with care!

Operational problems

Even if a camera does not have to move, it can be very tiring to operate its controls while crouching or kneeling for any length of time. It may be hard to see into the viewfinder properly, to focus and maintain good composition – particularly if lights are reflected in its screen. A further hazard of low viewpoints is that even quite low furniture (chairs, tables) can easily get in the way of the shot.

If you cannot lower the camera sufficiently to get the shot you want, it may help to use a mirror or a periscope attachment. But if the camera has to move around on shot, some sort of *low-angle dolly* or 'creeper' is the best solution. A typical height range for these special mountings is around 0·1 – 0·6 m/4in –2 ft. With a hand-held camera, even a castered board may help you to get the occasional low shot! For a stationary shot, you can fix a camera onto a *high hat* – a short cylindrical mounting, which can be bolted onto any firm surface (a board, box, or post).

Terms

You can get low-angle viewpoints by using a low camera position, by placing the subject higher than the camera or by shooting via a floor mirror.

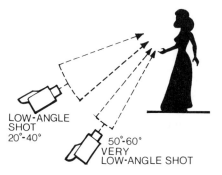

LOW-ANGLE SHOT 20°-40°

50°-60°
VERY LOW-ANGLE SHOT

Impact

Low-angle shots make most subjects appear stronger and more imposing.

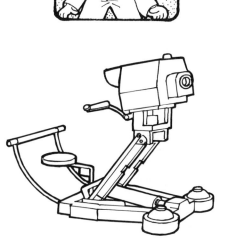

Low-angle dolly

Specially designed dollies are sometimes used when shooting continuous action from a low angle.

Dolly Shots

'*Dolly*' is the general term for any wheeled camera mounting. As this camera mounting moves to and from the subject, we *dolly in* (*track in*) or *dolly out* (*track out*).

Tracking lines
The dolly wheels can be steered in a straight tracking line, a curved track, or in an arc round the subject. As we saw earlier, *pedestals* can have two modes – *dolly* and *crab*. Where camera moves or camera positions are critical, you may find it helpful to draw discrete *guide marks* on the floor in removable chalk or crayon at strategic points.

The effect of dollying
Unlike the action of *zooming*, which simply expands and contracts the same image, dolly shots take us within the scene, passing various objects as we travel. We see the interaction of planes as the camera passes them, creating a strong illusion of depth and space.

Focusing
Having focused the lens at a particular distance, you will naturally have to readjust it as you dolly nearer and further from the subject. How critical focus readjustment is, depends on the *depth of field* available. (That you remember, relates to the lens' *focal length* and *aperture* and changes progressively with *distance*.)

The focus control rotates in one direction to focus *away* from the camera (*focusing back*), and the other direction to focus *towards* it (*focusing forwards*). How easily you can adjust the focus control while dollying, depends on its design and the amount of compensation needed to maintain focus. Some camera operators make continuous adjustments while moving; others refocus gently as the main subject in the viewfinder picture starts to 'go soft' (for a high-definition viewfinder should reveal unsharpness long before it is apparent on a TV receiver).

Floor surface
The floor of a TV studio is normally specially laid to provide a flat, smooth surface, over which cameras can dolly freely in all directions without risk of picture bounce. On location, where floor irregularities can cause problems, a camera may have to remain at a fixed viewpoint and rely on zooming to simulate dollying (moving to new positions while off-shot). Otherwise special lightweight dollies fitted with pneumatic tires (instead of the usual solid-tired wheels) are used for limited movement. Occasionally, special *floor rails* may be necessary, which allow the camera dolly to move smoothly over uneven ground.

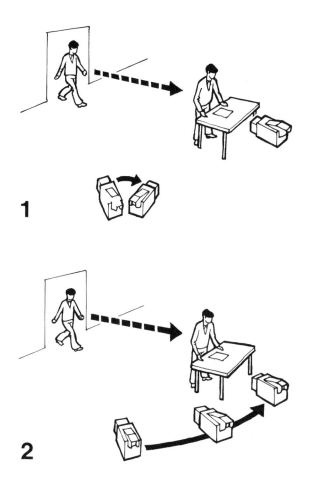

Fixed and moving viewpoints
When the camera *pans* around from a fixed position, the audience turn their
heads to follow the action. The director may then cut to a new viewpoint to
watch its continuation.
When the camera *moves* around, it changes the audience's viewpoint, 'walking
them over' to the new position in a smooth continuous movement.

Trucking and Arcing

Although simple enough in principle, it can take a lot of patient practice to provide smooth accurate lateral and arcing movements to order.

Methods of trucking (crabbing)

As a camera *trucks* (*crabs*) across the scene, subjects at different distances appear to pass each other – rapidly in the foreground, and proportionally slower with distance. This parallactic displacement creates a forceful illusion of depth; particularly where the scene contains many vertical features such as posts, columns, or trees.

Trucking alongside a moving subject (a *traveling* or *travel* shot) produces a strong impression of speed as background details slide past.

Some dollies are trucked by turning all their wheels sideways (as with the *crab* or *parallel* steering mode of a pedestal. Dollies that are steered by one set of wheels only (e.g. *camera cranes*) are 'trucked ' by dollying straight across the scene, with the camera head turned sideways.

Arcing

We usually move the camera round a subject in a tight circle —
• *To correct the composition* – When one subject is slightly *masking* (obscuring) another; e.g. in an *over-shoulder* shot.
• *To show the subject from different viewpoints* – For example, moving round a statue to show various features. After a knitter has spoken to the camera . . . it arcs round to watch their hands at work.

Operating problems

Some mountings move more easily than others. Where a *tripod dolly* or *rolling tripod* moves too easily, it can be difficult to control smoothly, and may truck quite erratically. Some *pedestals* are quite hard to push and pull when dollying/tracking, and tiring to truck over any distance. You may need the help of a second operator, to allow you to concentrate on focusing and composing the picture. When trucking with a pedestal at maximum or minimum height, assistance is generally essential.

Larger mountings such as *camera cranes* need a fair amount of space and time to reposition from a normal in/out tracking line, to *truck* across the scene. A really tight arc may be impracticable on some types of mounting.

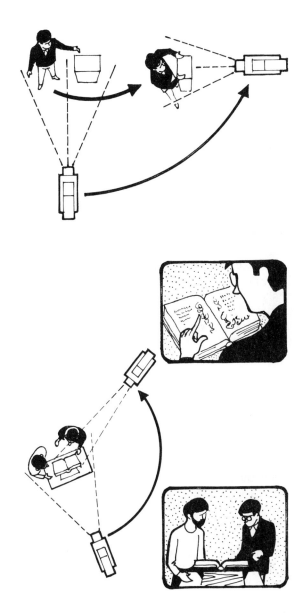

Moving subject
As the person moves to a new position, the camera arcs with him. The speed of the broad arc depends on how fast he moves.

Stationary subject
Here, having listened to the introductory conversation, the camera arcs round to see the subject itself more closely. The speed of this tight arc depends on the pace of the program.

Developing Shots

In a *developing shot*, the camera explores the scene as it moves on from one subject to another, or from one viewpoint to the next. It presents a smooth-flowing sequence of pictures, which build up an illusion of space and direction in the audience's mind.

You can use the developing shot for several purposes:

• *To establish location* – As the camera searches, it slowly reveals exactly *where* we are; e.g. panning past a series of items in glass cases, to establish that the scene of the action is a museum.

• *Realization* – The camera gradually introduces us to a *situation*; e.g. we see that the rising tide has cut off the travelers' escape.

• *Comparison* – Panning over a series of items in a collection, we can compare their style, color, etc.

• *To show relationships* – Demonstrating how one item relates to another; e.g. how far climbers have reached on a mountain.

Developing shots are frequently used when the mood is solemn or romantic. The pace (tempo) during the shot is unusually slow, for it is intended to encourage growing interest, or to build up tension. The big advantage of this type of shot, is that it avoids the visual disruptions of cutting between different viewpoints. There is a greater sense of audience involvement.

The mechanics of developing shots

Developing shots can involve very skilled, carefully controlled camera operation. As you move the camera mounting (dollying, trucking, arcing), framing and focus need to be corrected unobtrusively as the picture continually changes. Depth of field will vary. Not only must the camera move around smoothly, but you need to avoid any potential obstacles (e.g. furniture). It's important to avoid indecision, hesitation, uncoordinated movements or focusing slip-ups during a developing shot, for this would draw attention to the mechanics.

You may prefer to use a fairly *wide* lens angle for developing shots, as it makes handling easier and provides greater depth of field. But the camera would then have to work closer than with a *normal* lens angle – otherwise subjects would look too distant. There are also the hazards of distortion and shadowing problems. Certainly you should avoid a *narrow-angle* lens with its inevitable handling problems. And remember too, you will not have the opportunity to *pre-focus* any close-ups.

Try to use the same kind of dolly movement throughout. Changing from e.g. *dolly* to *truck*, is likely to cause the picture to bounce. Judiciously adjusting the lens angle instead, can simplify a dolly move; e.g. zooming in at the end of a long trucking move, rather than *changing the mounting's direction on shot* to dolly in to detail.

The varying viewpoint
The camera changes its viewpoint in a continuous exploratory movement,
showing various aspects of the action.

Camera Movement

The camera may need to move at speeds from an almost imperceptible 'creep' to a rapid dash – smoothly, accurately and safely.

Ultra-lightweight mountings
If a camera mounting is ultra-lightweight (e.g. a flimsy rolling tripod), camera judder or swaying shots during movement are not easily avoided; especially if the camera is much lower or higher than eye-level. Where possible, give the dolly a slight push in the appropriate direction while off shot. This aligns its casters, and avoids an initial jerk on moving.

Heavy mountings
Take care not to strain yourself when operating a studio pedestal that relies on heavy internal counterbalance weights. A rather cumbersome mounting, it requires some effort to get it moving and to stop. It's all too easy to damage nearby furniture, walls – or anyone in its path. Gentle foot pressure on the base helps to start a dolly move.

Controls
Where the left *panning handle* (*pan-bar*) has a central joint, some people prefer to have its end folded upright, rather than straight out horizontally. They can then reposition a lightweight mounting by pushing/pulling the handle end, while keeping the fingers of their left hand round the 'thumb-twist' *zoom* control. Their right hand is on the *focus* control – which may be on the other panning handle, or at the side of the camera head. This aproach avoids the need to leave the controls to push the pedestal's steering wheel. The result is less strain and greater control; and camera handling is easier for steep downward or upward tilts.

Points to watch
Unsteady pictures can give a highly dramatic sense of urgency to a news item, or suggest that someone is being jostled by a crowd. But your normal aim will be smooth, deliberate, unobtrusive camera handling.

It is best to continually check *focus* for maximum sharpness whenever the subject or your camera moves; rather than make obvious corrections whenever it becomes soft-focused. If both subject *and* camera are moving (getting closer or further away), *focus-following* will become correspondingly harder.

The speed of camera moves needs to be artistically appropriate too. *Slow dollying* can create gradually increasing interest. So it is most suitable for gentle, barely perceptible changes – in serious, thoughtful situations. But slow moves can also become tedious, boring, frustrating. *Fast dollying* can be dramatic and exciting – but can you stop at the end?

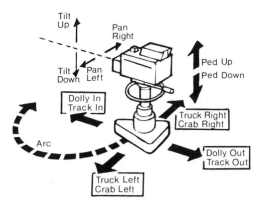

Camera movements

The camera head can *tilt* up/down, and turn to *pan* left/right. It can also be raised or lowered on its mounting (*elevate/depress*; *ped up/ped down*). The entire mounting can move forwards/backwards (*dolly* or *track* in/out), and move sideways (*truck* or *crab* left/right). Similarly, it can *arc* round a subject.

In the Field– The Single Camera

Four basic forms of *single-camera unit* are used regularly for *ENG, EFP, SNG*, and certain forms of studio production —

• The independent *camcorder*, where the video camera has an attached or incorporated videotape recorder, and produces videotape recordings for subsequent editing.

• The *stand-alone* camera which is cabled to a separate portable videotape recorder in a shoulder-bag, back-pack, or on a trolley-pack.

• The *stand-alone* camera working to a nearby support vehicle. That can be anything from a station wagon, remotes truck/van, to a mobile control room. The program material may be recorded there, or passed on directly to a distant control center.

The camera's maximum distance from its base largely depends on the kind of transmission link used:

Cable – *Multicore, triaxial, coaxial, or fiber-optic*. Each form has its particular practical advantages. Fiber-optic types are lighter, less bulky, more easily transported, easier to route (they can be suspended, wall-taped or buried), and can be used over much greater distances – e.g. up to 3000 meters (1·8 miles); about five times that of multicore cables.

Microwave link – Portable and camera-mounted video/audio relays.

I.R. link – *Infra-red* line-of-sight transmission to the base station.

• The *stand-alone* camera feeding a portable/mobile *satellite up-link* unit.

Supporting the camera

In the field, *shoulder-mounted* lightweight cameras are widely used for maximum mobility. But this method of supporting the camera becomes quite tiring after a while. Even with the aid of a *body-brace* it is not possible to hold a camera absolutely still, shot after shot for long working periods. When you have to use a *narrow-angle* (*long focus*) lens to get a close enough shot of the subject, your own natural movements can make a certain amount of unsteadiness unavoidable (heart beat, breathing, tired muscles).

Safety

If you are going to walk around while shooting, try to check your route beforehand for any obstacles. There are many potential hazards for the unwary, such as uneven ground, cables, rugs, stairs, low furniture, wet floors. Develop the habit of keeping *both* eyes open while looking into the viewfinder, so that you always remain aware of your surroundings.

Sound pickup

You can pick up sound on location with either a *camera microphone*, or a *separate* microphone held by someone else. (The latter can provide better and more consistent sound quality.) You can record the audio on a sound track of the videotape recording, or on a separate sound recorder. Time-code tracks help to identify and synchronize picture and sound. Although the picture will occupy most of your attention, if you are working unaided don't forget to continually monitor the sound, even if only on an earpiece. It may be catastrophic if you finish up with great pictures but unusable sound. And beware, the noise of footsteps walking across a gravel path may be your own!

Using a tripod

It may seem a chore to carry a *tripod* around, but unless shots are brief, you will soon welcome the stability it offers. A tripod can seem to develop a will of its own; so here are some hints for using them successfully:

• Tripods can become top-heavy and overbalance if their legs are not *fully* spread and properly adjusted, especially on uneven ground.
• Unless the tripod is very firmly based or bottom weighted, do not leave your camera unattended. If the pan-head is not tightly locked off, you may find the camera tilting and unbalancing the tripod.
• There are two kinds of ends to tripod feet: *spikes* that grip rough ground (but will pit, scratch, or slide on other surfaces), and *non-slip rubber endpieces* for smooth or easily-damaged floors.
• Always make sure that the tripod is level, and the camera correctly balanced. Apart from any built-in *level indicator*, you can check by locking the tilt action, and panning around. If the tripod needs leveling, horizontals will tilt down on one side (the leg that is too low).
• You should normally fully extend all three legs of the tripod. The exception is when you deliberately shorten a leg to suit uneven ground, rocky terrain, or a staircase.
• To improve a tripod's stability, and/or prevent its feet from sinking into the ground, fix its feet onto a special *spreader* or *base-plate*.

Videotaping and Editing

Using a *camcorder*, it is now feasible for a single person to shoot the entire production: the total picture coverage together with a complete soundtrack. But more usually, the camera operator is part of a small team; including a *director* who is responsible for organizing and selecting material, and someone who is handling the microphone and/or lights.

Methods of shooting
You can tackle an assignment in several ways:
• *Continuous recording* – Here you shoot an event continuously as it happens, choosing the best viewpoints available. Because you are recording everything, there is bound to be unwanted material in the final tape, but this can later be edited out as necessary.

• *Recorded sequences* – In this approach, you shoot an event in a series of separate segments; each 'video/sound bite' lasting perhaps 5 to 20 seconds. You might show the arrival of an aircraft for example, as –

The aircraft approaches... it lands... a stairway is attached... passengers alight.

Each shot presents only part of the entire process, but when edited together they build up an impression of the complete event.

• *Fragmented sections* – This kind of shooting provides a montage of very brief shots, each lasting for as little perhaps as 1 to 5 secs. It shows glimpses of action, places and things, which together build up a composite picture. Even a *continuous* action sequence usually consists of short diverse viewpoints, which edit together to look consecutive and quite natural —

Aerial view of a car travelling across a desert... cut to over-shoulder shot showing driver's view of the road... cut to a roadside viewpoint, panning as car speeds past... cut to head-on view through windshield of driver and passenger, etc.

• *Matching action* – When shooting drama and documentaries, action may be broken down into a series of short *takes* or sub-sequences. This can involve either:

Shooting the entire action as a medium to long shot and then repeating the action for certain sections to be shot in closeup, or

Repeating the action at the beginnings and ends of individual takes. This *matching action* will allow shots to be edited together smoothly to *appear* as continuous action. Otherwise overlapped, missed, or dissimilar action would be obvious when edited. In a simple example –

MID SHOT: Person approaches car, takes key from pocket, <u>inserts into lock</u>.
CLOSE-UP: <u>Inserts key into lock</u> ... and finds that it will not open.

114

Anticipating editing

Fundamentally, the *videotape editor* takes the recorded picture and sound – which is usually shot out of sequence – and copies appropriate sections onto a master tape to form the final version of the program. This is both operationally and artistically a very demanding process. Not only must there be continuity and unobtrusive transitions between sections, but the order and duration of each shot will directly affect its audience impact.

It is possible to shoot action so ineptly that the videotape cannot be edited together successfully, even if every individual shot is properly focused and perfectly composed! So let's take a look at ways we can help the videotape editor:

- Use an identifying slate before or after (inverted) each take.
- Keep a log with all shot details (including timecode). Label all retakes clearly.
- Shoot too much, and the tape can always be re-used. If you don't shoot enough, that material is *missing* and can't be replaced. The loss may ruin the scene!
- When shooting a sequence, there can be advantages in taking an overall *cover shot* or *establishing shot* of the scene, just in case it proves useful.
- Start recording just before the action begins, and continue after it has finished.
- Consider whether the start of a shot should match the end of the previous shot in any respect (*continuity* of action, clothing, direction, etc).
- Aim at maintaining continuity in the picture's *technical quality* (focus, exposure, color quality) and its *artistic character* (composition, headroom, panning speed, etc.).
- While shooting, look out for faults or errors and retake immediately.
- Shoot potential *cutaways* (e.g. traffic, pedestrians, bystanders) and record *wild-track sound* in case these are needed during editing.
- Take any close shots of details as separate *insert shots/detail shots* (e.g. jewelry).
- Consider whether special filters (e.g. sky filters, star filters) will enhance the shot, or whether such effects will be added later during post-production.
- Avoid either slight differences or extreme changes in size or direction, between shots of the same subject, that are to run consecutively .
- Start and finish a long panning shot with a '*held*' (stationary) shot.
- Don't re-record over a faulty take. Keep it in case parts can be used.
- When a sequence goes wrong, it may be better to retake it *entirely*. Otherwise, retake from a few moments *before* the error; not at the error point itself.
- Avoid *in-camera editing*; you may lose useful material. Edit afterwards.

Light and Lighting

Today's cameras seem to provide satisfactory pictures with almost any kind of lighting. So why do we need to introduce special lighting equipment? Well, the results when using natural or existing 'available light' are very unpredictable. Properly arranged lighting has important advantages:
- It allows the camera to produce optimum picture quality.
- It makes various features of the subject visible; revealing its form, texture, shadow detail.
- It can be used selectively, to show or conceal the features you choose.
- It can deliberately enhance or degrade the appearance of a subject or a scene.
- It creates an illusion of dimension, space and depth.
- It conveys an environmental effect. It creates an atmosphere.
- It can produce very consistent artistic quality, even when camera angles change.

Light intensities and contrast
Insufficient light, results in underexposed grainy ('*noisy*') pictures. If scenic tones are too contrasted, or there are overbright areas with deep shadows, the camera will not be able to handle the contrast range. You can accept this, keep the extremes out of shot, or light the shadows.

Avoid shooting into bright areas when using *auto-iris*. It will close, and underexpose the shot. Closing drapes over daylit windows, or changing the camera's position to exclude such surfaces often helps. You may have to place the camera to suit the prevailing light, rather than the best view of the subject. Perhaps you can angle the subject to suit the light.

Light direction
The *direction* of light considerably affects a subject's appearance . Always think of its angle relative to the *camera's* position. Whenever the camera or the light repositions, the pictorial effect changes correspondingly :
- Frontal lighting from behind the camera, suppresses surface modeling and texture.
- Side light shining across the subject will emphasize or exaggerate surface contours and texture, often creating a crude bisected effect.
- Back light pointing towards the camera will put a rim of light around the subject, to separate it from its background, and reveal any transparency or translucency.

Light from any angle will have some of these characteristics depending on which of these three basic directions it most resembles. As the *height* of a light source increases, modeling and downward shadows become increasingly harsh.

Color temperature

The light's color quality affects color fidelity of the picture. Orange-yellow light such as candlelight (*low color temperature*) is at the lower end of the Kelvin scale. Bluish daylight (*high color temperature*) at the upper end.

If your camera's color balance (red-green-blue proportions) does not match the prevailing light, the picture will have a *color cast* and appear unnaturally blue or orange-yellow. *White balance* (*auto-white*) circuits or corrective color filters will adjust the error, matching the system to either *daylight* or *tungsten* illumination – but not both. If several types of light are intermixed (e.g. daylight, tungsten, fluorescent) there will be color errors in surfaces lit by the uncorrected sources.

Light characteristics

There are two fundamental light characteristics:
- *Hard light*   – which casts well-defined shadows, creates modeling, and reveals form. It comes from concentrated (*point*) sources.
- *Soft light*   – which ideally is entirely shadowless, illuminating without casting any shadows. It comes from broad, large-area, diffused sources.

Most successful lighting is a blend of these two forms.

Basic lighting equipment

1. Reflector board – The simplest portable device used for supplementary lighting. Strongly reflected *hard light* from its shiny side; *soft* diffused light from its matte surface.   Useful for diverting sunlight onto a subject. Particularly valuable when shooting sunny exteriors, for a reflector will provide an effective key or fill light, yet use no power source.

2. Camera light (video light) – A small spotlight attached to the camera; (100 – 350 W).

3. Sun gun – A small hand-held spotlight directed by a second operator. Run from battery or utility power supplies; (e.g. 250–1000 W). May have a diffuser and corrective filters.

4. External reflector spotlight (lensless spot; Redhead; Blonde) – A lightweight spotlight supported on a collapsible extending tripod stand; (250 W, 600 W, 800 W).

5. Broad – A small trough light (500 W – 1000 W or more) which covers a wide area with comparatively soft light.

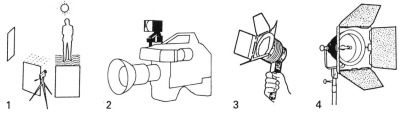

1   2   3   4

117

Remotes – Multi-Camera team

'*Remotes*' (*outside broadcasts*) cover situations ranging from sports events, exhibitions, conferences, to Grand Opera. So working conditions and venues can be extremely varied, including sports stadia, industrial locations, churches, theaters, golf-courses, etc.

While a studio camera crew usually works within sight of each other, a remotes unit may be dispersed over a vast area, each camera being isolated by the sheer scale of operations.

Location vehicles
Remotes vehicles can be anything from a compact two-camera truck to a mobile *production control room* with complete video and audio facilities, supporting six or more cameras. The unit may be used in various ways –

• Parked within an action area, with cables trailing out to cameras at vantage points.
• Used as a drive-in control room outside a temporary 'studio' (a public hall, theater).
• Its portable video and sound equipment may be removed and set up inside a building.
• Used with a small mobile stage or studio at the location site.

Camera distribution
Shooting inside a building can be similar to regular studio working; using pedestals/rolling tripods, a jib arm, or even a small portable crane. Cameras are often set up on tripods positioned at fixed strategic points (e.g. in a theater box). Shoulder-mounted cameras too, offer high mobility.

In the open air, cameras can be tripod-mounted in a wide variety of positions: on a *platform frame* (*camera tower*), *hydraulic lifting platform*, a balcony, even a roof-top . . . or down amongst the public on a sidewalk.

Initiative
In the field, there is always the unpredictable! Distant directors often rely on cameras' shots to reveal exactly what is going on out there! The show can largely depend on individuals' initiative in offering up those extra unanticipated shots – from the subtle gesture to the split-second drama of unexpected tragedy. Such pictures make a good show great!

Problems
Remotes cameras tend to use narrower lens angles (e.g. $20° - \frac{1}{2}°$) in order to get close enough shots. (In the studio $50° - 5°$ is typical.) So not only is depth of field reduced, but camera handling on movement can be that much more difficult. Increasing *drag* helps, but for subjects at extreme distances, or in windy conditions, it may even be necessary to lock off the panning head altogether, to hold shots steady.

Lighting conditions on remotes can change considerably; from intense sunlight needing ND filters and a small lens-aperture, to situations where the lens is working wide open to cope with low light levels.

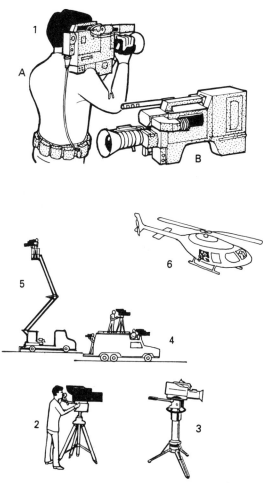

Cameras on location
1. Lightweight cameras powered from a battery belt (A) and camcorders (B) are widely used.
2. The tripod-mounted studio camera.
3. A lightweight camera mounted on a pneumatic tripod.
4. A mobile truck/van with hatch, roof and rear-platform cameras.
5. A hydraulic platform.
6. Helicopter camera.

Studio Production

Two or three cameras are sufficient for general purposes, although larger studio shows may use four or more cameras.

Facilities
The most comprehensive studio arrangements include:

- Production control room where the director watches the continuous output of all cameras, remotes, film channels, etc. on picture monitors. These video sources are fed to a production switcher (vision mixer), and switched (intercut) or combined as required.
- Audio control section where all program sound is monitored and adjusted.
- Lighting and video control where studio lighting and picture quality are controlled.

Production techniques
There are several different approaches to video production —
VIDEOTAPING:
Most shows are videotaped, and subsequently edited, to place items in order, omit errors, adjust durations, etc. In more elaborate *post-production editing*, program sound is augmented (*sound sweetening*), and video is treated (video effects, titling, picture correction added).

- *Live on tape* – The show is videotaped 'as it happens'. The cameras' pictures are selected and intercut at a *production switcher* during performance. Alternatively, each camera's output may be videotaped *separately*, and the tapes edited together later.
- *Recorded in sections* – Productions are often taped shot by shot, or a scene or act at a time (*rehearse/record*). This may be done in the final order (*running order, program order*), or in whichever order proves the most convenient for staging.

LIVE TRANSMISSION:
Here the production is distributed or transmitted *live;* although it may also be recorded at the time, for re-use or for archives.

Teamwork
While cameras at remotes can considerably help the director by 'offering up shots', in most studio shows where conditions are more predictable, shots usually follow a closely-knit scheme. Guided by a *camera card/shot card* and the director's *intercom* (*talkback*) instructions over a headset, each camera operator sets up planned shots. Ideally, all camerawork is closely coordinated; shots and camera moves are arranged to form a smooth-flowing presentation.

Multi-camera shooting
When several cameras shoot continuous action simultaneously, the director is able to cut between a variety of shots, follow widespread action, vary viewpoints, and combine shots. More important, particularly on a *live* show, is that all switching can be carried out during production, to provide *a complete production package* in a single session.

120

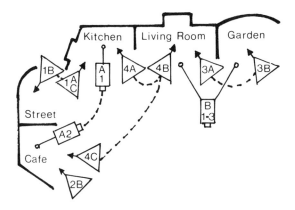

The camera plan
The positions of cameras 1,2,3,4 are successively marked (1A, 1B), and positions of sound booms A, B are shown as A1, A2.

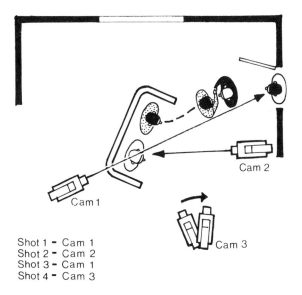

Shot 1 – Cam 1
Shot 2 – Cam 2
Shot 3 – Cam 1
Shot 4 – Cam 3

Multi-camera shooting
Each camera is allocated its shots: e.g. Shot 1 – Cam 1; Shot 2 – Cam 2; Shot 3 – Cam 1; Shot 4 – Cam 3.

Ready for Rehearsal

Here is a brief run-down of routine pre-rehearsal checks. Most will seem obvious... but that's when you start to take things for granted!

Studio Camera check-out

- *PRELIMINARIES*:
Camera switched on, warmed up and lined up?
- *CAMERA HEAD*:
Are panning handles firmly attached and at a comfortable angle?
Unlock the tilt lock and check the camera-head balance. Is it nose or back heavy? Check and adjust tilt drag (vertical friction). Unlock and check pan drag (horizontal friction).
- *LENS*
Remove the lens cap. (Switch lens electrical capping off.) Is the lens clean?
Check the *f*-stop number selected during the camera line-up with a chart under standard illumination.
Focus – Check focus control smoothness from nearest to furthest distance (*infinity*). In a lens servo system, is there any spurious focus overrun; any *hunting* (rhythmical changes) occurring? Focus at the widest (zoomed out; short focal length) and the narrowest angles (zoomed in; long focal length). Check that *focus remains constant* as you zoom throughout the full range (i.e. that it is *tracking* correctly).
Zoom: Is the zoom action smooth throughout its range? Check the *zoom indicator*. Adjust *shot-box* (if any) to preset lens angles and zoom rates. Check its operation.
Filters: Check filters (internal *filter wheel*). *Color temperature correction filter* correct.
- *VIEWFINDER*: *Controls* —Check focus, brightness, contrast, picture shape, edge cut-off, image sharpening (crispening). Are internal *indicators* working (zoom, *f*-stop, exposure, etc)? Are tally and indicator cue-lamps, meters, etc., OK? Check viewfinder's *mixed feeds*.
- *MOUNTING*:
Column – For a *rolling tripod*, check column height and adjustment. For a *pedestal* unlock column and raise/lower. Check its ease of movement and vertical balance.
Steering – Check free movement in all directions; in dolly (track), truck (crab) modes.
Brakes – On a rolling tripod check that individual caster brakes are OK.
- *CAMERA CABLE*:
Are the *cable plugs* at the camera head and wall (or equipment) outlet tight? Is the cable secured to the camera mounting? Is there sufficient cable for camera moves, and is it suitably routed for the show?
Adjust *cable guards* to avoid cable overrun or floor scraping.
- *INTERCOM* (*TALKBACK*):
Check intercom (general and *private-wire*), and *program sound*.

Preparing lightweight cameras

In addition to the above where appropriate, check the following:

- *VIEWFINDER*: Is the fitting secure? Check all warning lights and indicators.
- *MICROPHONE*: Is the microphone secure and working? Check connections, cables.
- *CAMERA LIGHT*: Is the lamp secure and functioning? Check light-spread and filters.
- *CABLE*: Do you have enough cable for the job? Has the camera's *cable correction* (*compensation*) control been set to suit the cable length used? Are *cable joints* firmly screwed together? Route the cable to protect it from feet, vehicles, etc. (Sling it, hide it, cover it over, or bury it, whichever is apppropriate, to the situation.)
- *BATTERY*: Check that the fitted battery and standby batteries are fully charged.

122

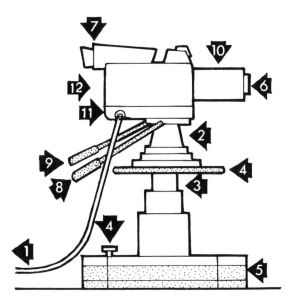

Camera checkout
Typical checkout points include:
(1) Camera cable. (2) Camera head security and balance. (3) Column.
(4) Steering. (5) Cable guard. (6) Lens condition. (7) Viewfinder. (8) Zoom
action. (9) Focus checks. (10) Lens aperture. (11) Intercom (talkback). (12) Shot
card (camera card).

123

Check the Studio

Before rehearsals start, let's take a look at some very worthwhile checks that can anticipate problems. First of all, identify the various *action areas*. Some will be self-evident: the office, the kitchen. But suppose there are several interview or performance areas? Which is which? Often they will be given identifying letters (e.g. *'Area A'*) or names.

Referring to your *camera card*, locate the various main camera positions and moves. Are there any obvious problems? Perhaps there is some obstruction just where the dolly will be operating. It does happen: insufficient room to get between two flats, some temporarily stored props, a lighting fitting in the way. Check around. Perhaps you can see that a spotlight on a stand outside a room window, will be in shot from one of your positions. Observation now saves time later.

Cable routing
There may be a single communal wall-box for all cameras' outlets; or duplicate points around the studio, allowing you to use whichever is nearest to your main action area.

In a major studio production the best floor route for your camera's cable to take as it runs from the wall outlet (plugging point) to each main viewpoint, is marked on the show's *camera plan* (*Camera 2* will be at positions *2A, 2B, 2C*, etc.). That avoids unnecessary cable runs stretching across the studio floor, impeding other cameras' movements.

Camera cables can get trapped under scenic flats, floor monitors or loudspeakers, furniture, etc. So make sure that you have enough free cable for your moves. Keep any surplus piled in a neat figure-of-eight coil in an out-of-the-way spot behind scenery. It is not only frustrating to strain against tight or snarled-up cable, but liable to damage the cable too.

Checking dollying areas
It's a good idea to look around the *studio floor surface* in areas where you will be dollying your camera. There may be odd obstacles during early rehearsal – ranging from cables (lighting, monitors), lumber used in last-minute construction, carpets, even wet floor paint – that could upset smooth dolly moves. The floor needs to be clean, too. A dropped cigarette butt has stuck to a dolly wheel before now, and caused camera judder!

Ready to go
Finally, let's move to the opening camera position. On with the headset, just look over the *camera cards* (*shot sheet*) or *run-down sheet*, focus up on the scene, and you're ready to go!

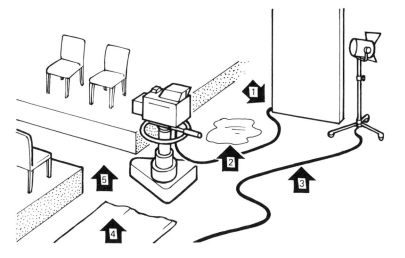

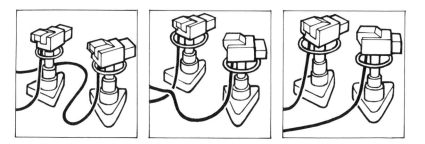

Floor check
There are often various problems for the unwary, including:
(1) Camera cable trapped. (2) Water on the floor. (3) Lighting cables that prevent
dollying. (4) Floor covering that frustrates a dolly move. (5) Scenery that
prevents camera getting into position.

Cable routing
In a continuous multi-camera production, it can be important to arrange camera
cables carefully so that they do not prevent dollying. Typical arrangements
include: working in another camera's loop, working under another cable (best
avoided) and parallel routing.

Camera Guides

How far directors plan and script production treatment, depends partly on the nature and complexity of the productions, and partly on their skills and temperament. Some shows need little preparation, others require detailed planning and coordination.

Where shot details cannot be predicted, improvisation may be unavoidable. But even complex situations can usually be broken down into a framework in which each camera has a prearranged selection of potential shots.

Some productions have a regular format, so that the director only needs to outline each camera's treatment;

> 'Camera 1 gives me a long shot for the opening of the show; mid-shot entrances and contestants, and close-ups of the panel as they contribute...'

Then it's up to each camera operator to be ready for these shots as they arise. Paperwork would be superfluous. Just make 'reminder notes'.

Camera script

A *camera script* contains a full record of the picture and sound treatment for the production. This is an essential document for production planning and reference, but is usually too detailed to be followed by a preoccupied camera operator, who uses abbreviated information sheets instead.

There are two forms of full script; one has a single-column layout, while the more comprehensive version uses two columns: the right half contains the dialogue (*lines*), stage instructions, action, lighting cues, sound treatment, etc. The left half gives details of which cameras are used, the shots required, and the switching (*cuts, mixes/dissolves, wipes*).

Information sheets

For simpler situations, an *outline script* may suffice, with brief camera and sound details, '*in and out*' cuewords for announcements, film and VTR inserts, etc. You may be able to use this as a '*camera card*'.

Breakdown sheet/running order/show format – This gives a list of various events or program segments in order. It shows camera and sound pick-up arrangements for each, the setting used, talent names, etc. (This list is sometimes inaccurately referred to as a '*rundown sheet*'.)

Camera card/shot card – A small card clipped to each camera shows its main positions in the settings, its allocated shots (numbers and types), the camera moves, basic action, etc. This is the main (or only) reference guide used by most operators in a busy multi-camera production, to supplement the director's *intercom* (*talkback*) instructions.

Shot sheet – A useful treatment summary list for unscripted shows, carrying brief details of all cameras' shots.

RUNNING ORDER

PAGE	SCENE	SHOTS	CAMS / BOOM		D /N	CAST
1	1. INT. WOODSHED	1 - 9	1A. 3A.	A1	DAY	Mike / Jane
3.	EXT. WOODSHED	10 - 12	2A.	F/P	DAY	Jane / Jim
	Recording Break					
4	2. INT. SHOP	13 - 14	4A.	B1	DAY	George
6	3. EXT. WOODS	15	1B. 3B.	A2	DAY	Mike / George
7	4. INT . SHOP	16 - 20	4A.	B1	DAY	George

CAMERA CARD

CAMERA ONE   ' THE OLD MILL HOUSE '   STUDIO B

SHOT	POSITION	LENS ANGLE *	SETTING
2	A	24°	1. WOODSHED LS TABLE PAN MIKE L. to window.
5	(A)	35°	MS MIKE moves R. to stove JANE into shot L. Hold 2-shot as they cross to wood pile.

MOVE TO POSITION ' B ' DURING SHOT 6.

21	B	10°	BCU door latch. ZOOM OUT to MS as door opens.
24	(B)	24°	CU back of MIKE'S head. As he looks up . . . TILT UP TO MCU of PAT (POV shot)

* OPTIONAL

In Action

All members of the camera and sound crew on the studio floor wear headsets. Through these they receive the general production intercom (talkback) and the program audio.

This may be a communal system, in which everyone on the intercom circuit is heard. In another arrangement, the studio team hear just the director and an assistant. Other production-team members (technical director, video engineers, etc.) use access-keys or separate private-wire circuits to talk to the crew. Cameras can reply over their headset microphones, or on a nearby studio microphone.

During rehearsal

It is best to keep instructions or discussion brief on intercom. A lot of unnecessary chat can be tiring to listen to. People tend to 'switch off' mentally, and assume that the verbiage is for someone else! The director guides the team over intercom:

> *'Camera 1, she will be moving in a moment, so start to pull out.*
> *(The lecturer stands.) She's going over to the table... you tighten as she gets there.*
> *Camera 2, a BCU of the vase as she points to the decoration... '*

During the take

By the time the taping session or transmission time arrives, intercom instructions have become brief action reminders, with the director's assistant calling out each shot number and camera, readying other sources (e.g. film channel), giving timings, countdown cues, etc:

> *'Coming to 1... On 1... Shot 15... Ready for the rise... Stand-by 2...*
> *Coming to 2... On 2... Camera 1 moves to the window...'*

From their camera card, each camera operator knows details of the camera's positions, type of shots, moves, etc. During rehearsal, each has learned the performer/talent action, the camera operations involved (panning, focusing, dollying). Now all that is needed is a brief reminder. The intercom system coordinates action, and alerts the crew to any particular difficulties.

Be prepared

Always keep a step ahead, by checking on your next planned floor position and its shots. As soon as your present shot is completed and the switcher has gone over to the next camera, try to move there silently, yet quickly.

When dollies move around fast, or travel over long distances, the noise of cable drag can be heard quite clearly in a quiet studio. A cable-handler (*grip, tracker*) can help by ensuring that the camera always works with a sufficiently slack cable loop, collecting together surplus cable, avoiding snarl-ups, taut or trapped cable and similar hazards.

128

Instructions		Meaning
Stand by 2: ready 2: coming to 2 . . . on 2, shot 40, camera 1 next		General guide procedure for cameras (used for general crew co-ordination).
Pan left (or right)	} head movement	Turn the camera head left (or right).
Tilt up (or down)		Tilt the camera head up (or down). 'Pan' often used, e.g. 'pan up'.
Centre up (frame up)		Arrange subject in centre of picture.
Focus up	} focus	Focus hard on subject (to a defocused camera).
Lose focus on . . .		Defocus subject named.
Split focus		Focus evenly between subjects (making both of optimum sharpness).
Follow focus on . . .		Keep hard focus on moving subject named.
Focus forward (or back)		Refocus nearer (or further away).
Defocus the shot		Defocus shot overall (usually by focusing forward to limit).
Give more (or less) headroom	} framing	Increase (decrease) space between head and upper frame.
Cut (or frame) at . . .		Compose picture to place frame at subject named.
Lose the . . .		Adjust framing to omit subject named
Stand by for a 'rise'		Be prepared for performer to stand up.
Single shot	} shot type	Shot containing one person.
2-shot, 3-shot, etc.		Shot containing number of persons indicated.
Group shot		Shot containing an indicated group of persons.
Close-up, mid-shot, three-quarter shot, etc.		Specific proportions of people filling frame.
Wide shot (cover shot, long shot)		General term for an overall view of action from that camera position.
Give me a wider shot		Use wider angle lens from that camera position.
Widen the shot a little		Usually indicates slight track back to increase coverage. May mean increasing zoom lens angle.
Give me a looser (fuller) shot; not so tight		Provide more space in frame around subject(s), i.e. longer shot.
Tighten the shot		Reduce space between subject and frame, i.e. closer shot.
Track in (dolly in)	} dolly movement	Move camera mounting towards subject.
Track back (dolly back)		Move camera mounting away from subject.
Creep in (or back)		Move camera very slowly towards (from) subject.
Crane left/right (also tongue, slew, or jib)		On a crane, swing the camera boom arm to left (right).
Crane up/down (also boom or tongue)		On a crane, swing the camera boom arm up (down).
Elevate (ped up)		On pedestal mounting, raise camera head (i.e. alter lens height).
Ped down (depress)		On pedestal mounting, depress camera head (i.e. alter lens height).
Tongue in (or back)		With crane base at right angles to subject, swing bottom arm to (from) it.
Zoom in (or out)		Narrow lens angle (widen lens angle).
Clear on three		Camera 3's shot is now finished. Move to next position. (Dismiss subject.)
Clear two's shot		Remove obstructions from camera 2's shot.

129

The Director Relies on You

Although there will always be those occasions when individuals have to make major decisions 'on the hoof', closely coordinated teamwork is the secret behind most first-rate producions.

How can you best fit into this team? Well, in a number of ways –

- Through your skills, accuracy, reliable operation, and dependability.
- By thinking ahead to avoid potential problems. Anticipating mechanics.
- By suggesting workable solutions when you have difficulties in getting the planned shots.
- Through flexibility. Be willing to try something, even when you are convinced that it will not work!
- By patience with repeated rehearsal, altered shots – even confusing instructions.
- By being consistent. Having a reliable memory (or make clear notes!) in order to be able to repeat shots and moves accurately.

Be adaptable

Don't let problem moments throw you! Perhaps you find in a live show, that there is not time for a planned move, or a shot is impracticable, or a dolly move needs to be changed. Be ready to compensate if someone is out of position (*off their marks*). Your initiative may prevent a disaster – but take care not to end up reorganizing the director's treatment!

It's not good enough to get a 'good shot'. Only the director has an overall picture of events, and each camera needs to relate to that treatment. If Tom on Camera 1 decides that a high shot presents the subject most effectively, while Dick on Camera 2 provides a powerful low shot, and Harry on Camera 3 goes into screen-filling close-ups, the consecutive shots would not intercut! Shots have to be rationalized and related, to have continuity.

Using initiative

Seated in the production control room, the director is often unable to look out onto action on the studio floor, and has to rely on what the monitors reveal. When problems arise (such as a sound boom preventing a camera from moving in closer), a wide shot from a nearby camera can be an invaluable help in sorting matters out quickly.

In unrehearsed, impromptu or unpredictable situations, you may be able to offer up unanticipated shots from your viewpoint. Your solution to a problem may save valuable rehearsal time. But take care. Instead, it may frustrate other cameras' shots, and ruin planned lighting and sound treatment!

Confirming the shot

Make sure you are getting the required shot. These are all *two-shots* but each has quite a different audience impact.

Correcting shots

When errors arise, do what you can to compensate. In this case the right-hand person has not walked forward sufficiently to hit the floor marks. The camera moves round to improve the shot.

Lining Up Your Shots

The trick is not only to get succesful shots during rehearsal, but to repeat them during taping or when the show is on-air, despite the tensions and complications of working under pressure.

When people are immobile – sitting behind a desk for example – it is easy enough to repeat the same shot. But in a dynamic situation where they are moving around, with groups forming and reforming, accurate composition under these changing conditions can be quite critical.

Repeated shot accuracy

There are a number of techniques you can use to ensure that you get the same shot each time:

• *Check your lens angle* – Because your zoom lens is variable, you need to make sure that it corresponds with the angle (or focal length) you used during rehearsal. (Perhaps noting it on your camera card.)

• *Check 'landmarks'* – Look at each shot carefully, to see where the frame 'cuts' objects in the background. These clues help you to remember the original composition.

• *Check surrounding space* – What is *nearly* coming into shot? There may be a bright window to avoid. Are you almost *shooting off* the set (*over-shooting*)? By anticipating shot limits, you will not be caught out.

• *Check the dolly's floor position* – A quickly made *floor mark* can show exactly where the camera was positioned in rehearsal. But only make marks that you can remove easily after the show (lumber crayon, chalk, adhesive marker tape). Do avoid very conspicuous or excessive marks. (Performers also need footmarks.) They can be confusing, and may be visible if that part of the floor appears in shot.

You can often use parts of the setting or the furniture to help you locate a camera position accurately: e.g. 'Just at the end of the wall, or beside the bookcase'.

Why bother?

Some people rely solely on their 'photographic memory' and spurn any aids. They are the ones who seem to encounter unexpected lens-flares, get those camera shadows that weren't there last time, and finish up with different composition. Their guesses are less accurate than they believe!

You can easily find yourself working at a different distance from the subject than in rehearsal, then having to use a different lens angle in order to try and compensate. The shot's proportions will be different!

Dolly over to a position that is 'roughly where you were last time', and you are likely to find that background features now look noticeably different behind the subject. A tree is now growing out of the singer's head, that was not there before! That is why so many experienced camera operators insist on lining their shots up methodically.

Floor marks

Mark your basic floor positions carefully, always using the same part of the dolly as a guide. In a multi-position show, lettered marks can relate to your camera card. Avoid using too few or too may marks. This may only confuse you.

Shot coverage

Check your lens angle. Look around to check what is just in shot and what remains just outside the frame. By doing this you can repeat the rehearsed shots exactly during 'transmission'.
If the shot omits items that were originally included, or now shows extra items, its impact changes.

Nearby subjects

Keep an eye on what is happening in vicinity. People may move into shot accidentally. You may find that just a slight camera movement brings unwanted things into shot.

Matching Shots

As an audience watches the screen, they see a sequence of carefully selected intercut pictures telling a story. But if the show you are working on is shot out of final order, you may have little idea how your particular shots are going to be edited into this complex jigsaw puzzle.

A well-made show has continuity of styles and techniques. Even where shots have been taken on different occasions or by different people, they need to intercut as a smooth-flowing continuous effect.

In a multi-camera crew, individuals have to rely on the director's guidance to ensure that their shots blend with others. Otherwise, left to themselves, a crew might choose excellent but almost identical shots, or present unrelated pictures that would not intercut successfully.

Avoiding spurious effects

Whenever cameras are shooting similar subjects, it is possible to get some very strange effects when intercutting between them. Switching between differently-sized pictures of people, can cause them to 'grow' or 'shrink' on the transition. Mix between similar shots of two people, and you produce astonishing 'Jekyll and Hyde' transformations. Fine when you want that effect, but otherwise it can be quite distracting!

It is important to maintain *consistent headroom*. When it differs noticeably in successive shots, or when the camera heights vary, the visual jumps on cutting can be visually disturbing.

Although these are mainly matters for the director to worry about, you do need to be aware of them, so that your shots fit in with those from other cameras.

Matched shots and mixed feeds

There are situations where you want to match your shot as accurately as possible to another camera's, so that the two pictures combine very exactly. If for example one camera is showing a map, and another has a graphic of town names which are later faded up and superimposed. Or again, in a combined shot, where one camera shows a choir, while another has a small localized insert of a soloist. If they are mismatched, the result could be disastrous.

Many video cameras have a *mixed feeds* switch which allows you to superimpose another selected camera's shot onto your own viewfinder picture. You can then adjust your framing and image size to make the two shots match. Without this facility, you would need to watch a combined picture on a nearby studio picture monitor, or be guided into position from the production control room.

Accidental effects

As the director cuts from one picture to another, visual mismatching can create disturbing effects.

1. *Height jumps.* Caused by mismatched lens heights that have no dramatic purpose.
2. *Headroom changes.* Shots have different amounts of headroom.
3. *Size jumps.* If the subject changes size slightly on a cut, it creates the effect of instant growth or shrinkage.
4. *Transformations.* If shots are very closely matched, one person can seem to become transformed to another on the cut!

Shooting Unrehearsed Action

Rehearsals are important! It is the production team's opportunity to judge whether their ideas and organization are going to work out. The director wants to check action, performance, shots, sound, lighting, staging and the various other contributory elements as fully as possible.

Preparation
Some situations simply can't be rehearsed – because the performers will not be arriving before the recording session, or you are shooting a once-only event, or because the situation is quite unpredictable (especially where animals or children are involved!). However, instead of just positioning cameras and hoping, an experienced director devises a flexible plan of campaign that will cover the best options, and can be adapted as circumstances allow.

Many forms of production such as interviews or panel games, follow such a familiar pattern, that the director just outlines the general format of the show, and briefly indicates the coverage of each camera.

A few simple precautions can ensure that presentation is smooth-flowing. Let's imagine that a group of politicians is going to be questioned by members of a studio audience. If everyone is allowed to talk at random, the camera and sound crews are going to spend a lot of time searching around to locate each speaker. By the time cameras and microphone have reached them, they may have finished! Wherever possible therefore, it is better if people speak in an order agreed beforehand, or give a clear signal before joining in.

It helps too, if speakers or characters in a show are clearly identified for the team. It is embarrassing to be asked for a close-up of Jo, only to find that you've picked Joe by mistake!

Methods of approach
There are two general methods of tackling unrehearsed action:
- Allocating particular types of shot; e.g. Camera 1 takes *wide shots* (*cover shots*) of the area, while Camera 2 concentrates on *closer shots* as they become available.
- A director isolated in the production control room, may have to rely on the initiative of camera operators to see shot opportunities from their viewpoints. These off-the-cuff '*grab shots*' can be quite successful, as long as cameras do not just concentrate on items that interest *them*. A series of shots of the visiting celebrity, with none showing the studio audience's reactions, would be very limiting.

The best technique for grab shots, is take a close shot of a possible area to *prefocus your zoom*, then zoom out to a wide view. Look around outside your viewfinder, checking for potential subjects. When you see appropriate action, zoom in for the director to assess it.

136

Area coverage
Cameras may concentrate on
certain areas, ready for action
there.

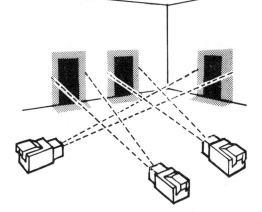

Localized coverage
Cameras may concentrate on
certain types of shot, moving to
fresh areas as directed.

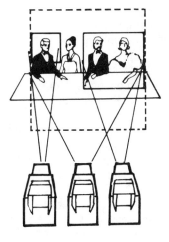

Unexpected action
By checking general action outside
your shot, you can see if you are
missing any important action.

Problems during the Show

When a production is on air *live* or being recorded *live-on-tape*, what is the best solution when problems develop?

• *'I've missed a shot!'*– If something prevents you from getting your camera into position and you miss a shot, try to get there as soon as possible. Don't risk missing the next shot too!

• *'The talent is out of position!'* – Even experienced performers sometimes fail to hit their rehearsed floor marks. All you can do is to reframe, adjust the lens angle, or reposition the dolly to re-compose the shot.

• *'He's moved into my shot!'* – Having set up your shot, someone (or something) suddenly intrudes into the picture. Occasionally you can ignore them, but otherwise it's a matter of reframing slightly away from the intruder, or gently tightening the shot to exclude them.

• *'It's too close to focus!'* – When someone comes so close to the lens that you can no longer focus sharply, you can only dolly back or widen the lens angle – or simply move the subject further away.

• *'I've lost focus!'* – If the depth of field is limited, and your subject suddenly moves out of focus, should you make a *gradual* or *immediate* correction? If the image is *slightly soft*, gentle refocusing is effective. But if the shot is badly defocused, it's probably best to correct it as quickly as possible.

Whenever you want to check that you have the sharpest focus, turn the focus control to and fro slightly (*rock focus*). Are *distant* subjects sharper than your main subject? Then you are focused too far away (*'focused back'*). If distant objects are indistinct and your main subject is soft, you are *'focused forward'* of the correct plane, so adjust focus the other way.

• *'I've got a lens flare!'* – Usually much clearer on a color monitor than in a black-and-white viewfinder. Solutions include taking a higher shot and tilting down a little; improving the *lens shade/lens hood*; shielding the light off the camera.

• *'My cable is trapped!'* – There's little you can do if you are on shot, except move around within the available cable length. Wait for an off-shot opportunity to clear the problem. Otherwise you can only vary the lens angle to substitute for dolly moves.

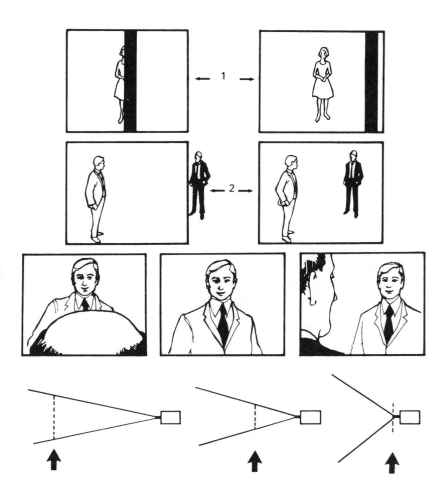

Wrong positions
A performer moves into the wrong position and (1) becomes masked by scenery (or another performer), or (2) is left outside the shot. By trucking (crabbing) left, the dilemma is resolved.

Sudden intrusion into the shot
If someone near the camera accidentally moves into shot, you can reframe the shot or move the camera to avoid them. Alternatively you can make them a definite part of the composition.

Minimum focusing distance
If a subject comes closer than the len's minimum focusing distance, you have to pull back, zoom out, move the subject further away . . . or let them go out of focus.

139

Helping the Talent

Whether an experienced actor or a first-time guest, the person in front of the camera has a sense of isolation – a feeling that now it's all up to them. Without taking on the role of a second director or bypassing the floor manager, the crew can help in various unobtrusive ways to put them at their ease. Even a regular professional's performance can fall off when faced with the 'cold turkey' reception of an indifferent floor crew. A friendly grin can be infectious!

Advising the newcomer
Many who appear in front of the camera are quite unfamiliar with television techniques, and are very willing to be told how they can help to get the best shots possible. Even an experienced demonstrator or interviewer may not realize that they are creating problems. That is where you can help, by showing them how they can assist you.

There are a number of regular hazards:

- They move an article around in a close shot, too quickly for you to follow.
- They accidentally cover over important detail when handling an article.
- They shadow detail in a subject they are showing.
- They move in front of the subject – *masking the shot.*
- They may need to angle a shiny subject carefully, to avoid it catching bad light reflections which distract or obscure (shiny book covers, glass covered pictures).
- For very close shots with a limited depth of field they will need to work within a restricted area, place things on a pre-arranged location mark.

Sometimes by sitting or standing in a certain way, or by hitting carefully located marks , a performer can help the success of a tricky shot, if you explain the situation.

Anticipation
One of the problems with inexperienced guests, is that they may not do the same thing twice! So always be prepared for them to move. Watch for the telltale hand and body movements which reveal that they are about to change their position, lean back, slouch, sit, or stand up. Otherwise you may be caught out as they pass out of the frame.

Remember the prompter!
Most performers/talent read their lines from a camera prompter. You can make life easier for them by ensuring that your camera is always within comfortable reading distance, and not so high that it forces them to look upwards into lights while reading.

Limited coverage
As the shot tightens, the amount of movement you can cover in this shot becomes more restricted.

Anticipating movement
Even experienced talent repositions without warning, or moves out of shot unexpectedly.

Helping Lighting Treatment

Whether you are shooting in the studio or on location, careful lighting treatment can make an important contribution to a production's success.

Altering the camera angle

If you decide to arc round a subject to what you consider a better viewpoint, and 'sell' this shot to the director, are you showing initiative or are you creating problems for others?

The effect that lighting has on any subject's appearance, depends not only on the angle and quality of the light (whether it is hard or soft), but on the direction from which you view the subject. Change your viewpoint, and its effect can alter considerably! A carefully angled backlight which was intended to produce an attractive rimming from the planned camera viewpoint, may now behave as a harsh side light instead! Altering lamps for this new unplanned viewpoint, could ruin the lighting treatment for previous shots.

The *set designer* too, who was not expecting the scene to be shot from this direction, may have to modify and re-dress the set to suit the new situation.

The *sound boom operator* may now have problems with boom shadows, when trying to pick up sound for this camera angle.

Remember, it's a lot easier to move your camera, or to rearrange the talent, than it is to change the lighting and scenery to suit new, unanticipated camera angles. Alterations take time, and may upset other shots.

Lighting hazards

Let's recapitulate typical aspects of lighting that affect camerawork:

- *Camera shadows* – The camera's shadow falling onto the subject, or being seen in shot (yours or another camera's). Slightly repositioning or lowering your camera may clear the shadow.
- *Lens flares* – Often not obvious in the monochrome viewfinder picture.
- *Spurious light reflections* – Direct reflections of lamps (particularly the camera light) in smooth background surfaces; e.g. glass, metal, plastic. They may be cleared by re-angling the surface, or altering the camera height. Otherwise surface treatment or re-lighting is necessary.
- *Shading in graphics* – When shooting graphics or title cards lit from above, adjusting camera height a little may avoid bottom shading.
- *Changing effective lighting angles* – Keylights are typically arranged at around 10° – 40° either side of a person's nose direction. If the camera trucks or arcs, and they turn to face your new camera position, their angle to the key alters, and the lighting effect is coarsened or flattened.
- *Lights appearing in shot* – Cameras can easily *overshoot/shoot off* into backlights behind the subject, particularly from low viewpoints.

142

Lighting matches planned shots
If instead of the planned position, 1, the camera moves to position 2 to imporve the shot, but can upset lighting treatment. Here the original backlight has now become a frontal keylight.

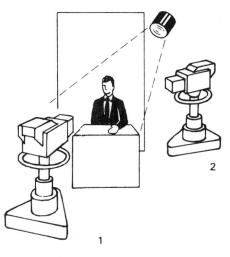

Camera shadows
If a close camera casts shadows on the subject, a more distant position with a narrower lens angle can clear the problem.

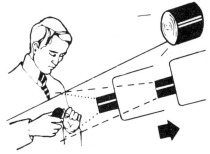

Lens flare problems
Lens shades (sunshades, lens hoods) for zoom lenses are most effective at the widest angles. At narrower angles, lens flares sometimes arise which can be cured by a temporary strip attachment.

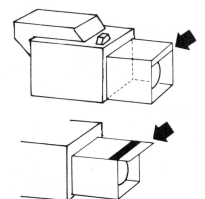

Helping Sound Treatment

For high-quality sound pick-up, the distance of the microphone from the subject is adjusted to suit the size of the shot – close sound for closeups, distant sound to match long shots and maintain *sound perspective*. Obvious enough, but often difficult to achieve.

Sound pickup techniques
Apart from worn *personal microphones*, the simplest type of mobile microphone mounting is the *fishpole* (*fishing rod*). Here the microphone is surrounded by a large cylindrical *windshield* (*windjammer*), and fixed at right angles to the far end of a light pole.
The sound operator's main aims are –

- To hold the microphone in a position that will pick up the best sound quality.
- To follow the moving performer.
- To avoid getting the microphone in your shot.
- To avoid microphone shadows being seen in shot.
- To avoid getting in the way of the cameras.

There are also two types of sound *booms*. The *small boom* (*giraffe*) is for stationary and semi-mobile situations, while a *large boom* is used in bigger studios for general action. They both consist of a horizontal arm, which is counterbalanced and supported on the center-column of a wheeled stand or mobile platform. The *boom operator* swings and extends the boom arm to place the microphone at exactly the right position for the sound source. Further controls turn and tilt the microphone as needed.

Camera and boom operators need to work together. When a voice is weak, the microphone will need to be much closer. That means your taking a slightly closer shot, to keep it out of the frame. Conversely, there will be situations when you need more 'air around a subject' than usual (e.g. in a wider shot). Then the microphone may draw back further away from the speaker than the ideal, so that it does not come into your shot.

Cooperation
To summarize then, you can assist the boom operator:
- By helping to keep the microphone out of shot – through careful framing, and by adjusting the headroom.
- By framing to avoid showing any microphone shadows cast on the scene or people.
- By coordinating with the sound-crew as they move around the restricted space on the studio floor.

Although boom shadows are largely a matter between the lighting director and the boom operator, you can often avoid or aggrevate the problem, depending on your exact dolly position and framing.

Keeping the microphone out of shot
The boom operator aims to hold the microphone as near to the talent as necessary, without moving into the picture or casting a shadow. The framing can be adjusted to help here.

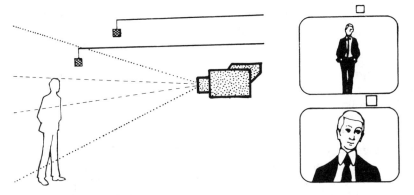

Matching sound and picture
The microphone is positioned to suit the shot size. Close shots need a close microphone. Longer shots need a correspondingly more distant position, to match the *sound perspective* with the pictorial distance.

Avoid shooting microphone shadows
By careful framing, you can often keep distracting microphone shadows out of shot as they fall on nearby backgrounds.

145

The Switcher and the Camera

Using the *production switcher* (*vision mixer*) in the production control room, the director can intercut or combine pictures from the various video sources (cameras, videotape, film, titling generators, etc.) in endless ways, as well as adding all manner of video effects. The actual switcher panel may be operated by the *production director*, a supervisory engineer (the *technical director*), or a specialist operator (*switcher, vision mixer*).

Helping the switcher

If you are working on a multi-camera production with rapidly changing shots and frequent intercutting between cameras, you need to have a pretty close rapport with the person operating the switcher to avoid mutual frustration.

In a fast-moving continuous production with few cameras, it takes a cool head to get each new shot quickly . . . hold it steady . . . focus and compose it in a moment or two, just in time for it to be switched to the main studio output (transmission) or videorecording channel.

If the switcher cuts *before* a camera is ready, the result is a bad shot 'on-air' (e.g. defocused, off-subject, moving into position).

If the camera is slow getting onto a shot, the action may have moved on by the time it is ready to be taken; e.g. someone at the door has now walked through it.

Watch the tally light

Whenever your camera's picture is switched 'on-air', a red *tally light* (*cue light*) is illuminated at the front of the camera with a corresponding indicator in the viewfinder. As the switcher cuts or fades to the next camera, these indicators go out, and you are free to move to your next setup.

It's particularly important to keep an eye on your tally light when your picture is being combined with *another* camera's, as any unplanned camera movements will ruin the combined effect – for example during *superimpositions, split screen, wipes, segmented shots, chromakey treatment.*

Whenever your shot is being *slowly mixed* (*dissolved*) to another, take care not to *alter* your shot in any way before the transition is over. The combined effect will become confusing if you move to your next position too early.

The switcher can help you in turn, by giving you warnings at difficult moments ('*Coming to 2* . . . *Still on 3* '), and by waiting for you to settle on a shot before taking it, when there has been little time for a quick move.

Settle shots quickly

Get to your shot as soon as possible, particularly in a fast-moving show. Until you have settled on your shot, the switcher cannot take it.

Wait to be cleared

Do not move to your next shot until your camera has been cleared, i.e. until the switcher has cut to another camera and your tally light (cue light) has gone out.

Any moment now!

The switcher can help the cameras by warning them that a shot is about to be switched on-air.

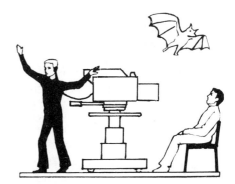

Shooting Graphics

Many graphics and titles are now generated electronically, but there are still regular situations where title cards, lists, maps, charts, tables, insert stills, etc., are set up in front of a camera in the studio for speed and convenience.

Graphics can be supported in several ways – on easels, caption stands, music stands, or attached to a scenic flat. They are usually mounted on thick black card. Typical sizes are 30 × 23 cm to 61 × 46 cm (12 × 9 in to 24 × 18 in).

Graphics are often just put into some available light and shot rather-casually. But perfectly good artwork can appear unsharp, distorted, shaded, tilted, with distracting light patches if it is not handled correctly.

Lining up graphics

Make sure that your camera is at right angles to the graphic, with the lens' *center-line* in the middle of the graphics card. Check that the graphic is *level* (horizontal) and not leaning back or sloping.

Is your shot appropriately framed? Is the complete graphic meant to fill the screen, or just a selected part? When you are shooting a title card, where is it to be placed on the screen; *centre-frame, head-title,* or *subject-title*? It may not be obvious. Is your title to be combined with another camera's shot (superimposed or inserted)?

Make sure that you are close enough to reveal all the required information clearly – but not so close that wanted information is lost beyond the television screen edges. Keep within the *'safe-title area'*.

If the graphic has a black background, the video engineer usually adjusts the video black level (*sets the picture down; alters sit*) to ensure than an even black tone is reproduced. However, to make it easier for you to frame the shot, it helps if the video is *set up* briefly, to gray-out the blacks and make the graphic's limits visible.

Light problems

Light reflections or glare can easily obscure parts of a shiny graphic or glossy photograph. If slight tilting or adjusting camera height does not remedy the problem, dulling with wax spray may help. Otherwise re-lighting may be necessary.

When you have to pan around a large graphic and move in and out to show details, zooming is much easier and smoother than dollying. But as you know, camera handling becomes coarser as you zoom in, and this can be obvious when you get in close to detail.

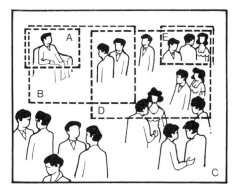

Title positions
Tilting can be located in several positions in the frame.

Shooting graphics
Graphics become distorted if they are not shot from a straight-on central position. Keystone distorton occurs if the camera is off-centre.

Exploring graphics
The camera can sometimes 'pseudo-animate' graphics by shooting them in sections, zooming in on detail, zooming out to take in larger areas.

Shooting People

There are very few productions in which people are not the main subject.

Single shot

In *'Basic shots of people' (page 68)* we saw the regular methods of framing a single person. But how you compose shots during a production depends on whether that person is speaking directly to camera or turned to face someone else –

- A *full-face* shot is usually framed centrally.
- A *three-quarter* frontal position has slightly offset framing.
- A *side-view* has much greater offsetting.

Two shot

As we saw earlier, if people are too far apart, you can often improve composition and reduce the central gap between them by arcing round a little to one side. You can also improve their relative proportions by altering the lens angle, and changing the camera distance.

Groups

There are a number of different ways in which you can shoot groups –

One-camera shoot:

- A single camera *continuously* shoots all the action, arcing round to new positions, zooming and panning between individuals as unobtrusively as possible (e.g. as a head turns).

  Avoid *whip-panning* between people wherever possible. It is far too distracting. An interviewer's questions are often shot separately, and edited in afterwards (together with *cutaway shots*) at points where the camera moved between shots.

- The single camera shoots *discontinuously*, and moves between several viewpoints. This means that you either *select parts* of the continuous action and miss out the rest, or the action has to be deliberately arranged to be shot in a series of *separate takes or sequences*.

Multi-camera production:

- Here the director shoots the action with a group of cameras, and either intercuts between relatively stationary viewpoints, or moves the cameras around to various positions while they are off shot. (While shooting impromptu action, a nearby *picture monitor* makes a useful reference point to avoid duplicating other camera's shots.)

Crossing the line

When shooting two people in conversation, always imagine a line cutting across the floor between them. If you *move* across this line while shooting, the audience will be able to follow the change. But if the director intercuts between different cameras *on either side of it*, people will appear to jump across the frame on the cut. This is not only distracting, but in more complicated groupings, it can cause the audience to lose their sense of direction .

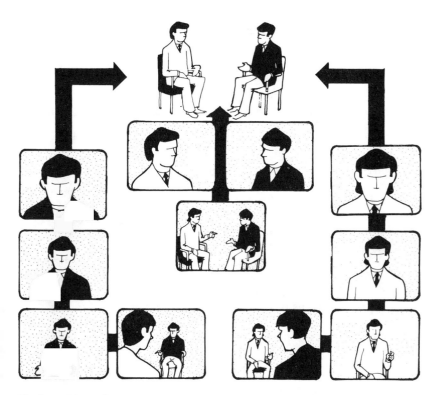

The formal interview
A number of 'standard' shots are used for most interview situations.

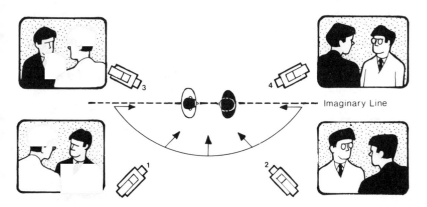

Imaginary Line

The 'imaginary line'
Shots can be intercut (cross-cut) between viewpoints *on the same side* of an imaginary line joining two people (1 & 2 or 3 & 4). But interswitching *across* the lines causes jump cuts (1&3, 1 & 4, 2 & 3, 2 & 4). There are no problems of this kind when *dollying* over the line.

Shooting Demonstrations

Demonstrations cover productions ranging from 'how things are used', 'how they are made', to 'how they work'. The camerawork involved is often exacting, particularly where very small detail has to be shown clearly.

Organizing close shots
The main difficulties with most demonstrations, lie in trying to –
• Shoot the subject from the optimum direction.
• Avoid getting in the way of the demonstrator (and *vice versa*!).
• Get close enough, and avoiding camera shadows.
As you would expect, depth of field limitations can be a major problem. When taking really close shots (e.g. filling the screen with something the size of a hen's egg), you may find focused depth so restricted that you can only focus sharply on one selected *part* of the subject. Although localized high intensity lighting would enable you to stop down, it could badly overheat the items being demonstrated.

Let's recap on ways a demonstrator can help you:
• By putting items on a pre-arranged mark.
• By not moving an object about quickly.
• By not shadowing or obscuring detail.
• By working within a confined area where necessary.
• By offering items up to the camera in an agreed order, rather than jumping between various items at random.

Whenever anyone holds an item up to the camera for a really close shot, you are relying on the steadiness of their hands, and on their holding it there long enough for you to focus and compose the shot before it is taken! If the situation is likely to arise, it might be as well to warn them during rehearsal; otherwise, you're taking a chance on shots of this sort. Particularly if you are going to zoom into detail, it is far better to shoot all big close-ups (such as marks on silverware) *separately*, and cut them into place during videotape editing.

Restricted depth
Some camera operators prefer to use a narrower lens angle for closer shots, for although depth is more limited and handling coarser, it avoids having to work too close to the action, distortion is not excessive, and there are no shadowing hazards.

When you are shooting displayed objects, *restricted depth of field* helps to visually isolate them against a defocused background. This not only concentrates the audience's attention, but tends to blur nearby distractions.

Viewpoint

If the viewpoint is poor, important detail may not be visible.

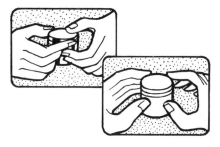

Table marks

If a demonstrator puts items down at random the camera may not have any good shot opportunities. Neat unobtrusive marks on the table can ensure that things are positioned accurately every time.

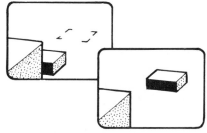

Steadying objects

If items are held in mid-air, pictures are likely to be unsteady and defocused.

Selective depth

Whether restricted depth of field helps (by isolating an individual item) or hinders (by not showing sufficient detail) depends on the purpose of the demonstration.

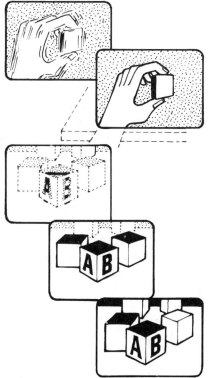

Shooting the Pianist

When you stop and analyze the range of regular shots you can take of a pianist at the piano, you will find that they are relatively limited. Of course, there are those various 'novelty' approaches – looking at reflections, silhouettes, and shadows. There are the 'unusual angles', and also those trick shots, in which pianists play duets with themselves or appear in multi-view segmented pictures. But unusual treatments have a nasty habit of drawing attention to their own cleverness, and away from the performer and the music itself.

A piano can be a challenging instrument to shoot attractively, for its large mass only frames successfully from certain directions. From other angles, the keyboard can't be seen – or even the pianist!

Optimum camera treatment
On the opposite page you can see typical shots a piano offers. Most effective views of the keyboard are shot from the right hand (treble) end, and put the pianist to the left of the picture. Shooting from the bass end of the keyboard, shots are rather restricted, for they do not intercut well with other viewpoints. There is always the danger of *reverse cuts*.

At normal camera heights, moving around the piano is confined to a rather limited arc, as the pianist's back, the piano lid or the body of the piano obscure the shot.

Depth of field problems
For close-ups of fingerwork, narrower lens angles are the obvious solution. However, depth is usually so shallow, that it may not be possible to follow focus on a fast-moving hand. Restricted depth, together with severe foreshortening of the keyboard, can make such detailed shots unpredictable.

Camera movement
Camera moves are generally keyed to the pace and mood of the music. Rapid shot changes from a variety of positions may be great for a pop group, but unless the director is prepared to have cameras in shot, operations can become too hectic to sustain. For a quiet passage during a recital of classical music, camera moves must often be so slow that they are almost imperceptible. The audience is not aware of the change, but they respond to the effect; the blend of sound and picture producing an emotional whole.

Top shot

Through lid

Over shoulder

Reaction shot

Hands

Along keyboard

Shooting the pianist
When presenting a piano performance, the basic range of attractive shots is relatively limited.

Shooting Instrumentalists

There is a great diversity of musical instruments, from piccolo to grand organ, from harp to percussion. Each offers a *very specific* range of interesting, meaningful shots. Some instruments are best seen in a wider shot, where both hands (and feet!) are busy with intricate action. In others the center of attention is comparatively localized, and only shown effectively in close shots.

Instrumentalists

Instrumentalists in a seated group tend to move very little, but solo performers frequently sway about as they play. Some violinists for instance, turn to such an extent that a single camera may not be able to sustain close shots of the fingerboard. Instead, the director has to alternate between several different viewpoints.

Shooting techniques should obviously suit the form of the musical performance. In *rock concerts,* off-the-cuff shots are intended for effect rather than to impart information. They convey the spontaneous spirit of the occasion. For more formal music, shots need to be selected carefully if they are to display techniques clearly.

Orchestras and bands

For orchestras and bands, camera treatment usually consists of:
- Wide shots of the entire orchestra.
- Group shots (sections).
- Shots of individual soloists.
- Detail close-ups of fingerwork.

Because large groups of musicians are spread over an appreciable area, cameras will normally be some distance from their subjects. So one has to use narrow lens angles for close shots, even if the resulting foreshortening is very noticeable.

Some directors favor continual camera movement between a variety of positions. Others prefer to intercut or mix between fixed positions.

Shot organization is important, otherwise there is every chance that a camera will arrive at an instrument just as its player has finished a passage, and is taking a dozen bars rest! Knowing the musical arrangement, and having a good memory for shots certainly helps. Although the director is probably following a score, a lot depends on individual camera operators' alertness.

As we saw earlier, there is always the temptation to take shots that are 'different' or 'dramatic': low viewpoints, reflections, floor shadows, rhythmical feet, and that old routine of focusing from harp strings through to the players beyond. Great ideas perhaps for suitable occasions – but make sure that they are appropriate!

Shooting the violinist
The shape of any instrument, and how it is played, determines which angles provide the best shots.

Filters and Effects

Shooting through a filter or an optical accessory can produce a variety of visual effects. Some are used for image enhancement, others as visual gimmicks. They may be clipped onto the front of the lens, or mounted in an internal *filter-wheel* within the camera head, ready for instant selection.

Neutral density filters – ND filters

Under very strong sunlight you normally have to stop the lens well down, to prevent over-exposure. But small lens apertures are not always desirable –
* Because camera lenses give better image quality at around $f/5·6$ to $f/8$.
* Because the resulting depth of field may be greater than you want.

By introducing a gray-tinted *neutral-density (ND) filter* which will cut down the light without affecting the picture's color quality, you can choose to work at a larger lens aperture.

Typical ND filters range from 10% (0·1) to 1% (0·01) *transmission*. Where bright lighting might normally force you to stop down to $f/16$ to expose the shot correctly, a 10% ND filter enables you to work at $f/5·6$.

When shooting under average lighting levels at $f/5·6$, an ND filter will allow another camera to work with *deliberately reduced depth at $f/1·9$*.

Where a shot includes a large area of bright sky at the top of the frame, this can affect the picture's overall exposure; causing the rest of the scene to appear dark. A *graded ND filter* will hold back the sky, so that the shot can be exposed correctly.

Colored filters

A *corrective color filter* can optically compensate for variations in the color quality (*color temperature*) of the illumination – e.g. filtering '*high Kelvin*' daylight, to match a camera system balanced to '*low Kelvin*' tungsten light. Otherwise the camera needs to be rebalanced electronically, by adjusting the camera's color channels, either manually or with *auto-white balance*.

Sky filters are vertically gradated, to add false color to the top part of the shot; e.g. to transform a plain uninteresting sky into a glorious sunset!

Effects filters

Star filters – Closely engraved grids on clear discs produce multi-ray patterns around light sources. Turning the filter rotates the rays.

Diffusion discs – These create effects ranging from slight softening to dense fog with haloed highlights. You can also fix nylon net over the lens.

Multiple images – Easily produced by multi-faceted *prismatic lenses* or by *multi-mirror kaleidoscopes*.

Distorted images – Shoot through ripple glass, a lightly oiled glass sheet, or via a flexible plastic mirror.

Prismatic lens
a multi-faceted lens provides several identiical images which can be rotated by turning the device. In the second type, the central image remains still as the peripheral images move around it

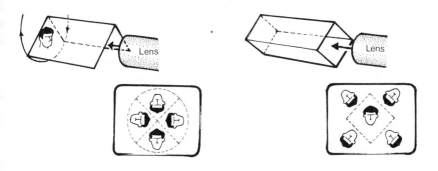

The kaleidoscope
Shooting through a three- or four-sided mirror tube produces an upright central image, surrounded by angled reflections.

All Done By Mirrors

You may want to shoot from an unusual angle for several reasons:
- To show details that are not normally visible (e.g. behind a statue).
- To get round obstructions that are blocking the shot.
- To shoot from a good but inaccessible vantage point.
- To present an overhead shot of the action – a 'bird's-eye' view.
- To show a subject from below – a 'worm's-eye' view.
- To achieve a dramatic effect.

Although today's small video cameras are highly mobile and adaptable, extreme camera angles can still pose problems. Studio cameras with their larger zoom lens systems and viewfinders, are considerably less flexible.

The direct approach
Perhaps you can place the camera exactly where you need it. But situations do arise where it would be quite impracticable to support the camera and its operator safely. A *remotely controlled* camera guided from a distant picture monitor could be the answer. A tiny preset camera can be positioned in the most unlikely spots! However, it may hardly be worth the trouble and expense of these expedients for an odd shot or two.

Using mirrors
The simple answer to many of these problems is to use a judiciously placed mirror; particularly where resources are limited. Instead of being tied up away from the general action, the camera can swing away in a moment to take normal direct shots.

Typical mirror shots include:
- Top shots of a demonstration table, using an overhead slung mirror.
  The camera, which is at its normal height, tilts up, and shoots via the mirror.
- A high-angle shot that would otherwise require a jib arm or camera crane.
- Level shots of a subject that is high up on a wall (statues, balconies, windows).
- Low-level and low-angle shots through a floor mirror or a periscope.

Problems with mirrors
Mirrors do have their drawbacks. The picture will normally be reversed horizontally or vertically unless electronically corrected (*line* or *field/frame* reversal), or unless you shoot via a second corrective mirror.

Glass mirrors take time and skill to rig and adjust, and need to be surface-silvered to avoid degraded double images. Lightweight mirror-surfaced plastic is quite satisfactory for some purposes. If the mirror is small or distant, its coverage may be too restricted. Overhead mirrors often obstruct lighting.

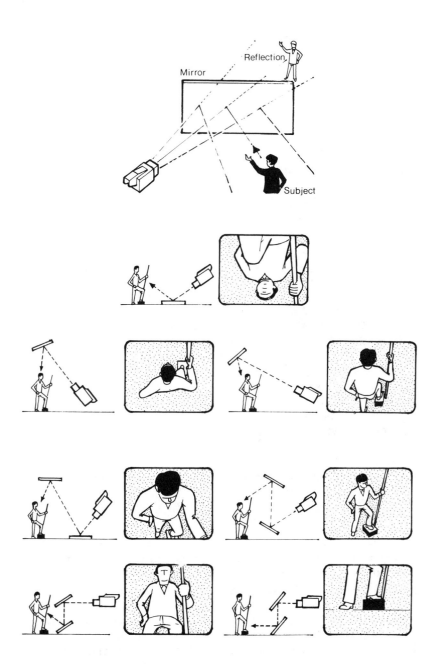

Basic principles
The reflected image is reversed laterally (side-to-side) and appears as far behind the mirror as the subject is in front. Focus on the subject image, not on the mirror's surface.

161

Camera Care

There is nothing more frustrating, time-wasting, and costly, than unreliable equipment that lets you down at a crucial moment. These camera care reminders can help you to avoid that happening.

The camera in use

During a busy day, it's easy to become a little careless in the way you handle your camera. A 'lightweight' shoulder-mounted camera can feel heavier by the minute after a long session, and it is a relief to put it down.

Remember though, your camera is really a delicate instrument. It doesn't like dirt, sand, sea-water, rain, moisture, hot sun, steam, mist, heat, extreme cold... The lens easily becomes coated with dust or condensation. Grit gets into tender parts, and can scratch as it is removed. It takes just a moment to protect your camera with a waterproof cover ('rain hood'). A brief oversight as a camera is rested on the ground, a spilt drink, the jolts and vibrations of a traveling vehicle can lay up endless trouble. A car's trunk can become an oven in hot weather. High humidity can wreak havok with videorecorders.

In short, it's a good general principle to fit your camera into a suitably protective container when you are not using it, or attach it to a firmly-based tripod. Care today, repays you with equipment reliability tomorrow.

When you disconnect or disassemble the camera, fix protective caps (or plastic bags) over cable connections, to prevent damage, damp or contamination. As you wind up the cable, take care to avoid twists and sharp bends. Dragging it over the ground can put quite a strain on it. A lot of 'don'ts' there, but bear in mind that any damage to the cable may not be obvious until you discover it the hard way – in use!

Batteries

Batteries too are often taken for granted. Make sure that you have all batteries checked and recharged after use. Don't leave them around in a half-charged condition. It shortens their life, and the running-time left in them is uncertain when you come to use them next time.

Batteries need to be charged correctly. NiCad cells can develop a 'memory' condition (depressed voltage) if you give them a long 'trickle charge', or over-charge and then leave them around partially discharged. If you use a battery for short periods (e.g. half an hour) and then recharge it fully, its voltage will appear maximum at first, but fall off after about half an hour, never delivering its full capacity. It is best to use a *cell discharger*, which drains the battery to a low voltage before recharging.

In cold weather, keep batteries warm in your pockets under clothing.

To protect the camera light, allow a freshly charged cell time to stabilize before using, for its initial voltage will be *high*, and it could 'blow' the lamp.

Routine checks

Human nature being what it is, routine checks become tiresome – but in the end they pay off. After switching off the camera at the end of a session, make it a regular habit to check out the following details:

• *PANNING HEAD* – Lock off and secure the pan/tilt movements. (Some heads have a securing chain.) Do not tighten drag controls. Has the head been operating smoothly? (Regular cleaning and lubrication is needed.) If weighty accessories (e.g. prompter, matte box) have been removed, check that the camera-head is not left 'back-heavy'.

• *PEDESTAL / TRIPOD COLUMN* – Lock off the vertical column movement. If a *prompter* has been removed, the column will now be wrongly balanced (harder to lower). It will need re-balancing if the mounting is used without one next time.

• *LENS* – Before attaching the *lens cover*, look across the lens surface against the light, Is it clean of dust and finger marks? Lenses have a very thin surface-coating (blooming) which reduces internal reflections, and improves picture contrast. This is easily scratched or worn, so never touch the lens surface. Use a special lens brush to dust it, or a can of compressed air. Only when these are ineffective, use lens tissues or lens-cleaning liquid.

• *CAMERA HEAD* – Is the camera head clean? Dust and grime soon build up. Have you had any mechanical or electronic trouble that now needs attention? Did the various *controls* operate correctly? (Focus, zoom, shot box, indicators.) Is the *viewfinder* OK? (Sharpness, brightness, linearity, mixed feeds, etc.) Is the *intercom* working properly? (Communal and private wires.)

• *CAMERA MOUNTING* – Have there been any problems? (Steering, elevation, motor controls, etc.) Check over the dolly's general cleanliness, including tire surfaces. (Odd remnants of plastic tape etc., get picked up, and can cause bumpy dollying; any oil/grease can cause tire-slip.) Check cable guards to ensure that they are not loose, too high or too low. Wheel brakes OK?

• *CABLE* – Having made sure that the equipment is switched off, remove the camera cable. Check that its ends are protected (capped) and store it neatly ready for next time. Typical methods include a figure-of-eight pile on a canvas carrying sheet, or a cable drum. Finally, place dust covers over the equipment.

• *STORAGE AREA* – Many studios simply leave cameras grouped on the studio floor at the end of the working day. If however, scenery has to be moved in and out of the studio, it is safer to have a nearby equipment storage room, away from the general traffic.

Practice Makes Perfect

There's a great satisfaction in being able to operate a camera reliably and effortlessly. But this precision only comes through practice. So we've included a number of exercises here, to help you to become familiar with typical camera moves. Do them slowly at first, building up to faster versions later. Videotape your efforts, to check your progress. A combination of these operations would test even the most experienced operator.

Some basic exercises

- Pan across a detailed wall surface (e.g. brickwork) at a very slow constant speed using wide, normal, then narrow lens angles, at different distances; keeping it in sharp focus throughout. Now tilt up/down slowly at a constant rate. This will give you the 'feel' of lens handling at different focal lengths.
- Pan across a scene containing a series of objects at different distances from the camera. Focus on each in turn: (a) pausing at each object; (b) quickly refocusing while still panning. Try this at different speeds and distances.
- Focus hard on a close foreground subject. Then tilt or pan to a distant subject, refocusing as you do so.
- Alter your camera height while keeping the subject exactly center frame. (Mark the picture center in your viewfinder if necessary.) Go from maximum to minimum camera height at different speeds. Shoot closer and closer subjects.
- Dolly in towards a newspaper pinned to a wall, continually refocusing for the sharpest picture. Use wide, normal and narrow lens angles in turn. Repeat the moves dollying out. Now try this with tabletop objects.
- Repeat these exercises, zooming instead of dollying.
- Truck (crab) the camera across the scene from left to right, then from right to left. Focus on objects at various distances as you move. Repeat the move, keeping one subject exactly in center frame throughout.
- Arc right round a stationary object, keeping it exactly center frame, using wide, normal and narrow lens angles.
- Without prefocusing, take a close shot of a nearby object, then tilt up and zoom in to some distant detail. Prefocus on the distant object and repeat.
- Set up a series of identical objects (e.g. playing cards, drink cans) in two parallel lines away from the camera. Dolly down this 'avenue'. Then zoom to simulate dollying. Note the differences (proportions, relative distances).
- At various camera distances, alter the lens angle so that the subject size remains the same. Note how the apparent sizes and distances of other objects appear to change.
- At 150 mm (6 ins) from the end objects note the MFD and depth of field for different lens angles.

164

Shooting people

If you can enlist the help of one or two others, there are some regular situations that are well worth practicing —

Distortion and depth
- With the lens *zoomed out*, move up to a person until you have a *close-up*. Check the sharpness of the background and geometrical distortion of the face. Repeat with the lens *zoomed in* to a *normal* lens angle. Compare the effect. Finally, *zoom in*, and pull back until you have a *mid shot*. See the differences. If you take a *head shot*, you will find that the results are staggering!

Following movement
- Follow a person walking across the scene from left to right: in a *long shot*, then in a *mid shot*, and finally a *close shot*. Repeat this from right to left.
- Have someone walk slowly towards the camera from *long shot* to a *close-up*.
- Have them walk diagonally towards the camera (far left to near right) following an uneven left / right path.
- Try all the above using different lens angles and camera heights.
- With the person in the distance, zoom in until you have a mid shot. As they walk forward, zoom out to keep their image size constant.
- Have a person walk away from the camera slowly as you dolly after them, keeping the same shot size. Repeat the action walking *towards* the camera while you dolly *backwards*. (Take care!)

Shooting two people
- Take a two-shot of people at different distances from the camera — e.g. at 2 m and 4 m (6·5 ft and 13 ft). *Zoom right out*, and check the depth of field available. See how far the focus control has to be turned to pull focus between the near and the far persons. *Zoom in half way*, and pull the camera back until the person in front is a similar size to previously. Repeat the depth of field and focus checks.
- Two people stand talking. Have one of them exit the shot, and – Hold the frame still. Notice that the picture now looks unbalanced? Reframe the shot unobtrusively (without zooming in), to centralize the person left.
- Have a single person center frame. As the second person joins them, zoom out and reframe the shot to correct the composition.

Obviously there are innumerable permutations on these exercises, but these are the stepping stones to smooth, reliable camerawork. When you have mastered these mechanics, you will be free to concentrate on the deeply satisfying process of using your camera as a creative tool.

Further Reading

If you want to explore further aspects of television/video production in greater detail, the following books by Gerald Millerson are available from Focal Press.

The Technique of Television Production, 12th edn.

An established standard textbook used in universities, broadcasting organizations, TV and film schools throughout the world. This is a detailed practical discussion of the mechanics, techniques and aesthetics of the medium. It explains the power to persuade and the nature of audience appeal, and includes a detailed analysis of picture composition and camerawork.

Video Production Handbook, 2nd edn.

A realistic practical guide to low-cost video program-making, that explains how to achieve professional standards with limited facilities and a restricted budget.

Lighting for Video, 3rd edn.

A rapid guide to practical lighting techniques in video and television production.

The Technique of Lighting for Television and Film

An internationally established sourcebook, discussing in detail the principles and techniques of the art of lighting.

TV Scenic Design, 3rd edn.

A study in depth of the art, mechanics and techniques of scenic design for television and video production.

Effective TV Production, 3rd edn.

A concise overview of the entire process of making television/video programs. It summarizes the practical and artistic essentials of good camerawork.

Glossary

Acting area The area within a setting where action takes place.

Action Any performance in front of the camera.

Action line (imaginary line) If shots from either side of an imaginary line connecting two subjects are intercut, the direction of the action and performers' positions are laterally reversed (mirrored). See **Reverse cut**.

AGC Circuits self-adjusting the video and/or audio to a preset level (strengthening weak signals; holding back strong ones.)

Amp (I) Ampere. Measurement of the strength of a current flowing through a circuit. (Also sub-units – milliamps (mA), microamps (mA)).

Angle of view The coverage of a lens; its horizontal and vertical angles.

Asymmetrical balance A pictorial arrangement in which a larger object close to picture center is balanced by smaller object(s) near the screen edge.

Aspect ratio The proportions of the screen: For regular TV, 4:3 (1·33:1). For Super 16mm TV film, 1·66:1. For HDTV, 16:9 (1·77:1). Some TV cameras can switch between the 4:3 and 16:9 standards.

Audio dub Replacing the soundtrack of a videotape recording with new audio program.

Auto-black balance Circuitry automatically adjusting the picture's darkest tones to a preset black level.

Auto-exposure Circuits adjusting the lens aperture and shutter speed to correctly expose the picture technically. May be able to be locked or manually controlled.

Auto-fade An in-camera facility for gradually reducing a picture's intensity to black at the end of a shot (either by closing the iris, or reducing video gain).

Auto-white balance Circuits automatically recalibrating the camera's color balance, to suit changing light conditions. Inaccurate where a single color predominates in the shot. Can be locked to a particular setting or manually controlled.

Back focus The distance between the rear element of a zoom lens and the image sensor, at its shortest focal length (widest angle).

Back light Light directed behind a subject. Outlining the subject in light, separating it from its background and creating a three-dimensional effect.

Barndoor A *spotlight* fitting with two or four flaps, used to restrict the light beam's coverage. (Folding a top flap down, can prevent back light causing lens flares.)

Barrel distortion A form of distortion on a wide-angle lens, in which lines near the center edges of the picture bulge outwards.

Base station A central control unit for digital video cameras. Similarly *BSU (base station unit)*.

Battery DC power source in which chemical changes produce a standard electrical voltage. Power can be drawn until these changes cease (exhausted, discharged battery). Batteries used for video equipment are rechargeable. Typical cells include NiCad (nickel cadmium), lead-acid, silver-zinc.

Battery belt A series of NiCad batteries carried within a pocketed waist-belt; typical voltage 12 V (10·5 – 17 volts).

Beam splitter A prismatic device that splits the lens image into three filtered paths – the red, green and blue components of the scene's colors.

Bean bag Sometimes used to support a lightweight camera which is resting on an uneven surface.

Blocking Working out performers' positions, moves and action, relative to the setting and cameras' positions.

Bloom (block off, crush, burn out) When an excessively light surface reproduces as a blank white area; due to over-exposure, or the video hitting the system's maximum limits.

Body brace A strut or framework pressing against the chest, or into a belt, to help steady a shoulder or hand supported camera.

Boom shot (crane shot) A high-angle shot taken from a jib or camera crane.

Burn-in Titling or timecode information that is 'solidly' imposed on a picture. Also An image of a bright area retained temporarily or permanently on a *camera tube*, defacing subsequent pictures.

Burning When an excessively bright light is focused onto the camera's image sensor, that area may be destroyed. Although CCDs are far less vulnerable than camera tubes, sustained focused sunlight can damage them.

Cable correction Electronic correction circuits that compensate for the progressive loss of the highest video frequencies as a camera cable's length is extended.

Cable guard An adjustable vertical metal strip attached to the base of a dolly, to prevent floor cables from being overrun or trapped beneath its wheels.

Camera angle Broad term for the vertical or horizontal angle of the camera's viewpoint relative to the subject (high angle, low angle).

Camera cable The cable connecting the camera head's circuits to the remainder of its associated electronic equipment (e.g. CCU). It carries video, power, scanning and synchronizing signals, intercom, etc.

Camera card See **Shot sheet**.

CCU (camera control unit) In an analogue video system, a central video control unit from which most of the circuitry providing power, scanning and sync signals, etc., is distributed. Adjusted and controlled by an operator (shader) or video engineer to ensure consistent camera performance.

Camera sled A low-angle dolly.

Camera light (video light) A small lamp attached to the camera head to provide local illumination close to the lens. Used as a 'key light' in underlit situations, or as 'fill light' to reduce contrast and illuminate shadows in lit surroundings.

Camera tube An electronic vacuum tube type of image sensor, with a light sensitive surface (*target*) which is scanned by an electron beam to generate a video signal.

Canted shot (tilted shot) A dramatic visual effect (created optically or electronically), in which the picture's verticals lean over to left or right, to suggest instability

Capping-up Placing a cover (*lens cap*) over a lens to protect it from accidental damage or excess light. Electrical capping-up, similarly places the electronics in a standby mode.

Caption General term for a graphic or title set up before a camera.

CCD (Charge coupled device) A solid state image sensor superseding camera tubes as a device for generating video pictures.

Cheating Changing the position of any item in between shots (person, object, scenery) in order to improve the composition from another camera angle.

Chinese dolly The combined effect of pulling back (*dollying back*) and panning, along a tracking line angled to the subject. Typically a frontal view of the subject that progressively becomes a rear view as the camera moves past.

Chroma key (CSO) Electronic equipment for inserting a 'subject' with a special color background (usually blue) into any video 'background', to create a seamless composite.

Color bars An electronically generated test signal comprising vertical bars of standard primary colors: white, yellow, cyan (blue-green), green, magenta (red-purple), red, blue, black. Used for checking cameras and other video equipment.

Color terms *Brightness (luminosity)*: the impression of the amount of light received from a surface. *Hue*: the predominant sensation of color. *Luminance*: the true measured brightness of a surface. *Saturation (chroma, intensity, purity)*: a pure undiluted hue has 100% saturation. Paled out with white, its saturation falls to a tint below this figure (e.g. pink at 15%). *Value*: the subjective brightness of a surface.

Color temperature A measurement in *Kelvins (K)* of the color quality of a light source. To reproduce color accurately, the color balance of the video camera and the prevailing light must match.

Convergence The accurate superimposition of the component red, green and blue images in a television display device. (In a camera tube, termed *registration*.)

Convertible camera A camera in which selected modules (lens, viewfinder, VTR,) are combined to suit a particular application.

Cover shot (protection shot) A wide-angle view of action, usually showing general activity from which other cameras are selecting specific detail.

Crabbing (trucking) Sideways movement of the camera mounting.

Cradle head A heavy-duty camera mounting head.

Crane arm See **Jib arm**.

Crash zoom A very rapid zooming action.

Crop To cut off. A shot framed to omit subjects or parts of subjects near its borders.

Cut An instant visual change, as one camera's picture is replaced by another's.

Cutaway A separate shot introduced within a main sequence, to deliberately interrupt its continuity (e.g. shots of the crowd during a game to disguise missing or omitted material, editing cuts, etc.).

Cut-in A shot interjected within the main action. Often used when parts of the action have been repeated and shot from another angle, or with a different shot size.

Dedicated VTR An arrangement in which each camera has its own associated videotape recorder in a multi-camera shoot.

Defocus dissolve (defocus mix) During a mix between two shots, one camera defocuses, while the other which was defocused, sharpens on its shot.

Depth of field The range of distances over which things appear to be in sharp focus.

Depth of focus The extent to which the distance between a lens and a light-sensitive surface (e.g. a film) may be altered and still maintain a sharp picture.

Detail shot A cut-in shot showing particular detail otherwise not clearly visible.

Developing (development) shots A continuous exploratory shot which moves around different viewpoints, to show various aspects of the action or the scene.

Diascope An illuminated device containing a slide of a TV test pattern, that may be attached to the front of the camera lens to assess the system's performance.

Differential focusing Positioning the focused plane so that a chosen subject is sharp relative to defocused surroundings.

Direction, camera Subject directions are usually referred to relative to the camera; hence '*move the vase camera left* '.

Dockable Detachable units fixed to a camera head (battery, VTR).

Down stage Towards the camera. See **Up stage**

Electronic cinematography camera (ECC) A video camera designed with mechanical and electronic features that provide performance similar to 35 mm cine cameras, and produce typical 'film look' picture quality.

ENG (electronic news gathering), EFP (electronic field production), ESG (electronic sports gathering) Names given to various types of production using lightweight video cameras in the field. See **SNG**.

Establishing shot An opening shot (usually an overall view) which reveals the location, relative positions, establish atmosphere, etc.

Exposure Adjusting the brightness of the image falling onto the CCD, so that scenic tones are reproduced with particular values. Usually by adjusting the lens aperture, but also by altering light levels, or using ND filters.

Eye line The direction in which a person is looking (or appears to be looking).

Favor To give greater prominence to one person than another in the same shot.

Fill light (filler) A light (usually diffused/soft) intended to illuminate shadow and reduce contrast, without casting additional visible shadows.

Filter A transparent material placed over or behind the camera lens to modify the lens image in some way: alter image clarity, change color values, affect exposure, etc.

Filter wheel A multi-opening disc within a camera, into which corrective or effects filters can be placed for instant selection. A blanked-off section 'caps up' the camera.

Floor manager A member of the production team who supervises production activities (responsible for floor personnel, discipline, safety, scheduling), relays the director's cues and instructions to the talent. (The camera and sound crew hear directly on intercom.)

Floor marking Chalked, crayoned, or taped marks indicating the positions of cameras, talent, furniture, scenery.

Focal length The distance between the lens system's optical center and the image sensor (CCD) when focused at infinity (far distance).

Follow focus To maintain focus on a subject during movement (of subject or camera).

Follow shot Dollying alongside a moving person, keeping a constant shot size.

Foreground The part of the scene nearest the camera.

Formats, camcorder Designs include both *analogue* (i.e. continuously variable signals) and *digital* (regularly sampled) systems. The video signal may be in *composite* form (total video information including syncs) or *component* form (luminance and chrominance signals kept separate).

Frame jumps If two adjacent cameras shooting the same action have a subject common to both shots, it may appear on the left of one shot, and the right of the other. Then it will appear to jump across the frame on intercutting between the cameras.

Framing Adjusting the subject size in a shot, relative to the picture area. Hence 'tightly framed' subjects fill more of the screen, and 'loosely framed' subjects less.

Gain The amount of amplification of an audio or video signal (*gain control*). *Video gain* may be increased to strengthen the weak video signal resulting from low light levels.

Gamma A logarithmic measurement of reproduced tonal contrast. It relates the brightness of subject tones to the equivalent tones in the picture. '*High gamma*' pictures have high contrast (crushed shadows and highlights). '*Low gamma*' pictures contain subtle half-tones over a more limited overall tonal range.

Gassing The adjustment of gas pressure in certain designs of lightweight pedestal mountings, to vertically balance the weight of the camera, prompter, etc.

Genlock A facility allowing individual pieces of video equipment (e.g. cameras) to be synchronized by a communal sync generator, so that all units scan in unison.

Grip In TV an operator (*tracker*) responsible for moving larger camera dollies, and cable control. In Film, an operative who assists the *gaffer* (responsible for lighting rigging), moves the dolly, is involved in setting camera rails, and may assist other technicians.

HAD (Hole accumulation diode) A form of CCD image sensor. (Also *HyperHAD*).

Hard focus Sharply focused. Opposite of *soft focus*.

Headset Worn by camera and sound crew; one earphone/earpiece carries *program sound*, and the other *intercom (talkback)* or *private line (PL)* information. A small attached microphone enables the operator to talk to production and engineering personnel when necessary.

Hyperfocal distance When the camera is focused at its *hyperfocal plane*, everything between half that distance and *infinity* (the furthermost distance) will be in acceptably sharp focus.

Hydraulic lifting platform A truck-mounted hydraulic platform which can raise the camera from e.g. 1·8 – 26 m (6 – 85 ft) above the ground. Used to support high cameras for *remotes* (e.g. golf matches), or mount high *microwave dishes (radio links)*.

Image intensifier An electronic lens attachment enabling a camera to provide monochromatic pictures at extremely low light levels (e.g. 0·2 lux – moonlight).
Imaginary line See **Action line**.
In-camera editing Operating a camcorder so as to deliberately join shots together *while shooting*. This technique produces program material that requires no further editing, but in practice it is inflexible and lacks finesse.
Insert shot A brief shot introduced during a sustained shot or sequence; e.g. as a *cutaway* or *detail shot*.)
Intercom (production talkback) Circuits enabling the director and production team to intercommunicate with the studio crew, unheard by the talent or the studio microphones. *Reverse talkback circuits (private line, PL)* allow operators of cameras and a sound boom to contact the production control room.
Interline transfer (IT) CCD A form of CCD producing low smear, and low inherent background pattern noise over the picture.
ISO (isolated) camera An arrangement in which a separate VTR continuously records the output from one chosen camera. During a live remote, this can be replayed onto the program wherever necessary (for *replay inserts*, *cover shots*, or *standby shots*).

Jib arm A counterbalanced centrally-mounted beam, supporting a remotely controlled camera at its far end. This single-operator facility provides variable camera heights up to plus 3 m (9 ft), and can swing sideways over a wide arc.

Key light The main light illuminating a subject. (Supported by *fill* and *back light*.)
Knee The upper part of the camera system's exposure curve, in which the lightest picture tones progressively compress; and at maximum clip off to white. Some cameras have automatic knees *(auto contrast)* which self-adjust arbitrarily to picture contrast.

Lens angle The horizontal and vertical coverage of a lens. To find it for a lens used with a $^2/_3$ in. CCD: double the focal length in use, divide 8·8 by this figure. Find the *inverse tangent (arctangent)* of the result. Double this for the *horizontal* coverage angle.
Lens axis An imaginary line from the center of the lens system towards the scene, passing through the exact middle of the shot.
Lens flare A spurious colored blob or streak resulting from a bright light or reflection shining into a lens system, and being internally reflected.
Lens hood (sun shade) A round or rectangular tube fitted to the front of a lens barrel, to shield off direct light rays, where light is shining towards the camera.
Lens mount A device enabling the lens to be attached to the camera head. Typically it is a 1 in. or 0·66 in. screwed *C-mount*, or a 0·5 in. *D-mount*. Quick-release *bayonet mounts* require a partial turn of a locking ring. The standard *VL bayonet mounts* on camcorders, allow 35 mm. still camera photographic lenses to be fitted.
Light levels Light intensity *(light level)* is measured in *foot candles* or *lux*. A camera requiring e.g. 186 fc (2000 lux) at *f*/8, will need only 1·2 fc (13 lux) when the lens is opened up to *f*/1·8 and 18 dB gain, or only 0·7 fc (7.5 lux) at *f*/1·4.
Location *'On location'* – shooting anywhere away from the studio. Hence *'selecting a location '* is choosing a geographical site for a location scene. A *remote (outside broadcast)* is a program operation on location.
Loose shot A shot in which an appreciable amount of space is left round the subject.

Macro A lens setting providing high enlargement. Items can be focused very close to the lens surface (sometimes even touching it). 'Zooming' may adjust picture focus.
Matched (matching) shot Arranging subject size and position in one shot to match those of another camera's shot; e.g. to provide a mix-through transition comparing old and new versions.

Matte (foreground matt) A mask or vignette. A silhouetted shape (graphic, stencil or electronically generated) which enables part of a shot to be isolated and inserted into another picture.

Matte box A box mounted in front of a camera lens, to hold mattes (masks), gelatin filters, effects devices. It also provides an efficient sun shade/lens hood.

Matte shot (1) Part of a shot is blanked out, and filled in with part (or all) of another shot. (2) A shot in which a painted or photographic image set up in front of a camera obscures part of the scene and blends with it; e.g. appearing as a ceiling on a studio set.

Minimum focused distance (MFD) The nearest distance at which a lens can focus.

Mixed feeds Circuitry allowing a camera's viewfinder to display another camera's picture superimposed on its own, in order to compare or align shots. (Neither camera's video output is affected. It is purely a monitoring process.)

Monitor, picture High-grade video display equipment, providing accurate, stable, high definition pictures. (Program sound is reproduced through a separate audio system.)

Monitor sound A high quality sound system (loudspeaker, amplifier) used to judge audio quality, or to reproduce sound in the studio.

Motorized dolly A form of camera dolly in which electric motors control all movements (forward/backward drive, speed adjustment, craning, etc.) instead of manual effort.

Objective camera treatment The productional approach, in which the camera is an onlooker *watching* (not taking part in) the action. See **Subjective**.

Off stage Outside the staging area; beyond the setting.

On stage Within the staging area; towards the center of the setting.

Over-expose Abnormally bright reproduction of a subject. In extreme over-exposure, lightest tones crush off to blank white.

Over-scan Adjustment of the picture size on a TV receiver or monitor, so that the picture extends beyond the screen edges. Pictures look bigger, but peripheral information is lost.

Overshoot (shooting off) A shot seeing past the studio setting and accidentally revealing other subjects; e.g. overshooting the top of a set and seeing hung lamps.

Over-shoulder shot (OS) A shot including part of the back of someone's head, as it shoots the person or scene they are facing.

Panning handle (pan bar) A metal tube attached to the *panning head*, enabling the camera's direction to be controlled. Single handles may have an adjustable central joint. Some operators use two handles (either side of the panning head), held at arm's length.

Panning head (pan head, camera mounting head) Bolted to the top of the camera mounting, this device allows the attached camera head to pan and tilt, or to be locked in a fixed position. Ease of movement can be adjusted *(drag)*. There are several types.

Parallactic movement As a camera moves through a scene, distant subjects appear to be displaced sideways more slowly than nearer ones. We judge depth from this effect.

Pepper's ghost The camera shoots the subject through a 45° angled plain glass sheet. Reflected in the glass, a lit object to the side appears as a ghostly image. This device can also be used to reflect light onto a multi-layer graphic, to avoid inter-layer shadows.

Perspective distortion An effect in which the apparent perspective in the picture is greater or less than in the actual scene. It may be an accidental or deliberate effect.

Pick-up shot A situation where a person in one shot appears to continue speaking into the next, although the time or place has obviously changed. *Also* an inserted *detail shot*.

Picture noise A random speckling or 'snow' pattern, due to electronic circuit noise.

Point of view shot (POV) Subjective camera treatment, in which the camera shows the scene from a participant's viewpoint.

Polarizing filter A special plastic filter which can differentiate between light from different directions. It darkens blue skies, and kills reflections in glass/water/metal.

Post production Treatment of videotape program material after shooting has been completed. Editing, sound sweetening, tonal/color correction, video effects added, etc.

Prefocus Momentarily zooming in and focusing on a subject while off shot, in anticipation of a later *zoom in*. (To avoid focusing inaccuracies due to depth of field variations.)

Private wire A speech phone line between single individuals; e.g. camera to CCU.

Prompter A device attached to the camera head to provide a performer with visual cues or full script which they read to camera. From simple cards to a TV display of the script reflected on a 45° glass sheet in front of the lens. (*Teleprompter, Autocue.*)

Pull back To dolly or track backwards away from the subject.

Pull focus To refocus (usually rapidly) from a far subject to another that is closer.

Quick release A plate bolted beneath a camera head, allowing it to be rapidly attached to a panning head. See **Wedge mount**.

Reaction shot A shot showing a person's response to an event.

Registration The process of adjusting two or more pictures, so that they are exactly on top of each other (coincident); as when combining separate red/green/blue images.

Resolution The size of the smallest detail that a camera or videotape system can reproduce; measured in black-and-white vertical lines or maximum video frequency. *Typical high grade camera* 750 to 850 lines. *Hi-8* and *S-VHS* 410 lines. *VHS* 260 lines. *NTSC home receiver* 350 lines. *HDTV* over 1200 lines.

Reverse angle A shot showing a subject from the reverse direction; e.g. showing a person from full face, then from behind.

Reverse cut The effect seen when a subject points in one direction in one shot, but appears to face the opposite direction in the next.

Rise To get up; e.g. from a chair. A warning that a performer is about to stand up.

Safety harness Webbing straps worn by a camera operator on a high camera crane.

Safety lane (fire lane) A marked-off area around a studio's walls, free from scenery or equipment, to provide an emergency escape or access route.

Safe title area Area of the TV screen within which all important graphics information must be framed to avoid edge cut-off.

Segmented shot A shot made up of a pattern of two or more other shots.

Set (setting) An arrangement of scenic units to produce an overall design.

Setup (line-up), camera Circuitry adjustments of the camera's video level, white and black levels, gamma and color balance to proscribed standards. (In tube cameras, also registration.) In digital camera systems, a *memory card* may be inserted to automatically align cameras to a universal standard setup.

Shader An engineer/operator who remotely adjusts exposure and various video parameters (color balance, gamma, etc.) for the best or most appropriate picture quality.

Shoot-off See **Overshoot.**

Shot box A push-button unit that allows any pre-set lens angle to be selected on a zoom lens system. You can use a line-up chart to adjust it to specific angles.

Shot sheet A card/sheet clipped to the camera head, showing its shots, positions, etc.

Single-camera techniques Production treatment in which a single camera provides all or most of the pictures during a production.

Size of shot The proportion of a subject filling the screen.

Slate A small black chalkboard held up to the camera to identify each shot for reference. It may include a countdown clock or a *timecode* display to assist cuing.

SNG (satellite news gathering) Field cameras connected to *satellite up-link* equipment, for direct transmission to a news center.

Soft focus Slightly defocused.

Sound sweetening The final, post-production process of compiling and adjusting the program's sound: adding music, sound effects, etc.

Split focus A compromise focus setting when depth of field is limited and two subjects at different distances cannot both be sharply focused; both are left slightly soft focused.

Split screen A bisected picture. Its left half shows the left part of one camera's shot, and its right half shows the right-hand part of another's.

Spring-loaded head A design of fluid panning head, in which internal springs provide resistance (drag) to camera movements.

Stabilizer A device that suppresses random movement, judder, vibration, to provide a steady picture. Designs include: a camera support (*Steadicam-Jr*), a body harness (*Steadicam*), and an optical lens attachment (prismatic, gyroscopic).

Staging The process of designing and arranging scenery within a studio.

Staging area (setting area) The main area of a studio floor in which scenery may be positioned. (It is surrounded by the *safety lane/fire lane*.)

Subjective camera treatment Using the camera to simulate the reactions of someone within a scene; imitating their movements (e.g. pushing through a crowd, getting dizzy).

Superimposition (super) Fading up two cameras' pictures at the same time to produce a transparently superimposed effect.

Supplementary lens A clip-on lens that will increase or decrease the existing focal length (lens angle).

Switcher, production A video unit enabling the outputs from various video sources (cameras, VTRs, telecine, etc.) to be inter-switched, faded, mixed, inserted, etc.

Switcher, routing A central switching panel which connects various program sources to their destinations.

Sync pulse generator Circuits generating the various synchronizing pulses required to ensure uniformly stable picture scanning and consistent color values.

Tally light A small low-powered indicator light fixed to the front of a camera to show when it has been selected on the *production switcher* (i.e. 'on-air').

Technical Director (TD) Engineering crew chief, who may also operate the switcher.

Thirds (rule of thirds) A rule-of-thumb concept for arranging pictorial composition, in which the picture area is divided into thirds, and principal subjects arranged on this grid.

Throw focus To refocus (usually rapidly) from a close subject to another further away.

Tight shot A shot in which the subject fills or nearly fills the screen.

Tilt wedge A wedge-shaped attachment fixed to a panning head, enables the camera to tilt downwards at a greater angle than normal; e.g. when shooting down from balconies.

Time base corrector (TBC) A unit that removes inaccurate or distorted sync pulses from a defective television/video signal (e.g. during reception from remotes, or caused by videotape jitter), and inserts accurate ones to correct color and sync errors.

Timecode A signal counting elapsed hours, minutes, seconds, frames; incorporated during video or audio recording (may be added). The 8-digit display gives precise timing for identification and editing. *VITC (vertical interval timecode)* is used professionally and on some small-format camcorders. *RCTC (rewritable consumer timecode)* on Hi8.

Tracker (grip) An operator who pushes a dolly, controlling its speed and direction.

Tracking, lens Ideally the selected focus of a zoom lens should not drift while zooming.

Transmission (1) The picture(s) selected by the director at the switcher, and displayed on the '*transmission monitor*', to be recorded or transmitted.

Traveling shot Any shot from a moving camera.

Trickle charge Low current battery charging rate.

Trucking shot A dolly shot. Often used to refer to extensive dolly movement, particularly a *follow shot*.

174

Twin speed A videotape recorder capable of recording at *SP (standard play)* for the highest quality, and *LP (long play)* for double the running time (although with increased noise, and lower definition).

Under-expose Abnormally dark reproduction of subject tones. In extreme under-exposure, darker tones crush off to black.

Up stage In a direction away from the camera.

Video light A small lamp attached to a consumer camera.

Video control (vision control) The process of continually adjusting the exposure and electronic parameters of the camera system for optimum picture quality.

Vision mixer See **Switcher, production**.

Volts (V) The electrical potential of a power source. It may be *AC (alternating current)* which fluctuates in polarity, or *DC (direct current)* which is of constant polarity. An *AC* supply may be up or down converted by a transformer, and rectified to provide a *DC* source of supply.

Watts (W) The power used by an electrical device. To find the *power* consumed in *watts*, multiply the current flowing (in *amps*) by the *voltage* applied. (One *watt* equals one thousand *kilowatts*.)

Wall outlet (wall point) An electrical socket attached to a wall, into which the plug at one end of a cable is fitted (camera, sound, or lighting). The outlet is permanently wired to associated equipment.

Wedge mount A type of quick-release camera attachment, that slides into a wedge-shaped housing in the panning head.

Whip pan (swish pan, blur pan, zip pan) A very rapid panning movement, showing the scene clearly at its start and finish, but blurring all intermediate detail.

Wild track Atmospheric or environmental sound, recorded (usually without picture) as potential background effects to be inserted into a program ('*Atmos*').

Wipe (1) To demagnetize (neutralize) any part of an audio or video recording.

Also: (2) A picture transition in which one picture is progressively hidden by all or part of another.

Wrap up To finish activities; to clear away.